The Life That Is Grace

The Life That Is Grace

by JOHN V. MATTHEWS, S. J.

S.T.D., Mag. Agg. (Pont. Greg. Univ.)

THE NEWMAN PRESS

WESTMINSTER, MARYLAND

1953

Imprimi potest: John J. McMahon, S.J.
Praep. Prov. Neo-Ebor.
October 24, 1952

Nihil obstat: Edward A. Cerny, S.S., D.D.
Censor librorum

Imprimatur: Most Rev. Francis P. Keough, D.D.
Archiepisc. Archidioec. Baltimor.
February 25, 1953

The nihil obstat and imprimatur are official declarations
that a book or pamphlet is free of doctrinal and moral
error. No implication is contained therein that those
who have granted the nihil obstat and imprimatur agree
with the opinions expressed.

Library of Congress Catalog Card Number: 53-7493

Copyright, 1953, by
THE NEWMAN PRESS
Printed in the United States of America

FOREWORD

In this book the writer seeks principally to stress that sanctifying grace is our supernatural life, a life to be lived, a life of growth, a life in Christ.

For Scripture references the Douay version of the Bible is used except on rare occasions—and there the exception is noted.

We are happy to dedicate this work to the Immaculate Heart of Mary, the Mother of Divine Grace; and we pray that she may be able to use this book in enlarging her Son's kingdom, which is also her kingdom.

THE AUTHOR

CONTENTS

I. JESUS OUR LIFE-GIVER 3

II. NEITHER HUMAN NOR ANGELIC LIFE 7

III. A DIVINE LIFE 12

IV. WHY A LIFE? 16

V. WHY A DIVINE LIFE? 24

VI. WHERE IS THIS LIFE? 29

VII. THE COMMON VOCATION OF ALL MEN 36

VIII. A TWICE-GIVEN LIFE 42

IX. A NEW LIFE 48

X. AN INTERIOR LIFE 54

XI. A LIFE OF GROWTH 62

XII. AN ETERNAL LIFE 77

XIII. A SACRAMENTAL LIFE 82

XIV. A LIFE OF SONSHIP 102

XV. A CHRIST-LIFE 132

XVI. THE LIFE OF THE MYSTICAL BODY 157

The Life That Is Grace

CHAPTER ONE : *Jesus Our Life-Giver*

Men risk danger to life and limb for different reasons—among others, for the sake of gain or the thrill of adventure. It is his pay envelope that keeps the "sandhog" working dangerously on a new subway. For the love of gain the diver risks his life beneath the sea to find some sunken treasure. The glory of sending home the best pictures and news is what makes the photographer and the reporter face death on the battlefront. Or it may be adventure that stirs a man to live dangerously. There are men who for the sake of adventure climb the world's highest mountains. They dare death and they know they are daring death. Then there are the hunters of big game. These men brave the claws and the teeth, the speed and the power of wild beasts; nevertheless, they risk injury and death gladly for the sake of adventure and the thrill of danger.

Thus men and women dare death for many reasons;

3

and we admire the courage of such persons. Yet there are even greater men and women whose deeds of devotion draw not only our admiration but our love and thanks as well. These are the heroes who in duty and love dare death to save the lives of other men. Not for gain or pleasure or adventure do these men offer to sacrifice their lives but only through devotion to and love of their fellow men. Indeed, so great is their love for mankind that, in trying to save the lives of other men, these heroes are ready to accept even their own death. "Greater love than this no man hath, that a man lay down his life for his friends." [1]

Surely we all know of this generous love. The policeman who plunges into the icy waters to save another man's life certainly risks the loss of his own life. The hero who leaps in front of a speeding train is seeking to save a human life but he is surely risking death for himself. Mothers risk their lives for the sacred purpose of giving life to their own flesh and blood. St. Aloysius dared and accepted death while doing his part to save the lives of the plague-stricken in Rome. Again we read every so often of the man who drives his automobile into a tree to avoid killing someone. Truly such heroes defy death to save another from death; truly such heroes love their fellow men.

We shall give one more picture of the man who dares even death itself to save the life of some other man. In 1900 Walter Reed, United States Army doctor, was ordered to Cuba to search for the cause of the deadly yellow fever. After some time he felt that the bite of a

[1] John 15:13.

4

certain mosquito caused the disease. Because animals would not take yellow fever, Reed called for volunteers. Many were the heroes who took the tests, and among them were two named Kissenger and Moran. Reed asked them, "But, men, do you realize the danger?" "We know. We volunteer solely for the cause of humanity and in the interest of science." Reed mentioned money. The two heroes answered, "The one condition on which we volunteer, sir, is that we get no compensation for it." Certainly these men were heroes. Certainly they risked life itself. Certainly they dared pain and fever and death. Not for pleasure or adventure or money or honor, but only to keep other men from dying of yellow fever did they themselves face death; only to save human life did they risk their own lives. They were true heroes, true savers of human life.

We have now seen our human heroes. Let us, then, turn to Him whom with love we call our Savior. For, like the heroes we have reviewed, Our Lord too dared death to save the life of man.

The bringing of that life to mankind was the reason why the Son of God took human flesh and became Jesus Christ. Everything Jesus did was for that one sacred purpose of saving life. Like a true hero, Our Lord risked even His own death in order to be the lifesaver of mankind. From His first moment in the manger He willed to bear cold, ingratitude, labor, weariness and insult; and lastly He chose to accept His own cruel death. All these hardships and sufferings Jesus bore as our lifesaver, for such was the strong desire of His loving Heart.

Indeed, Our Lord had dedicated Himself to the work

5

of bringing life to mankind. Jesus was a consecrated life-saver of men. Never did He forget this holy purpose, approved by His eternal Father. Our Savior was to embrace death in order to save the life of man. Hence Jesus was always the victim, destined to give up His own life that He might give life to us. Thus He told His followers "that the Son of man shall be delivered into the hands of men." [2] It was hard for the Apostles to believe this, yet always Our Lord preached His saving death. "Therefore doth the Father love me because I lay down my life. . . . I lay it down of myself and I have power to lay it down." [3] So, too, when some were angry at Mary Magdalen for anointing Our Lord, He said: "She is come beforehand to anoint my body for the burial." [4] Yes, Jesus would and did die; and back of this destiny was the grand purpose of His life and death: "I am come that they may have life and may have it more abundantly." [5]

In truth Our Lord is mankind's greatest lifesaver. For He is our divine lifesaver, our consecrated lifesaver. He said: "Greater love than this no man hath, that a man lay down his life for his friends," [6] and then He chose to lay down His life for us. Like a hero, He gave up His own dear life that He might bring us life.

With full right, then, do we call Him lovingly our Savior.

[2] Luke 9:44.
[3] John 10:17–18.
[4] Mark 14:8.
[5] John 10:10.
[6] John 15:13.

6

CHAPTER TWO: *Neither Human nor Angelic Life*

THERE are many different kinds of life in existence. Below human life there is the unthinking life of the flower and the beast. Above man there is the brilliant life of the angel; and, lastly, beyond all created life there is the divine life of God Himself.

Our Savior came to earth in order to bring life to man. "I am come that they may have life." [7] What life did Jesus give to us, His fellow men? What life did Our Lord's agony and scourging win for us? Our Savior set His Sacred Heart on giving us a certain kind of life, and that was His greatest concern in all His works. What exactly was that precious life which His Sacred Heart desired, first of all, to give us?

Clearly, Our Lord was not interested in giving us any life below man's own life of body and soul. For men can lower themselves to the level of beasts by their own power; man can make a beast of himself despite and

[7] John 10:10.

without the grace of God. Any hint that our Savior helps man to degrade himself would be a terrible insult to our Savior and our God. Indeed, exactly the opposite is true. The Son of God took flesh precisely because men were living like beasts and because He wanted to lift man out of and above that degrading life.

But if Our Lord would not give us a life below the human, neither would He bring us a merely human life. He was truly concerned with the bodily welfare of His fellow men. To the dead He gave new life of body. By restoring speech, eyesight and hearing He gave a fuller bodily life to the dumb, the blind and the deaf. To the sick Jesus gave fresh life; to lepers He returned the healthy life of the body. In short, His many miracles show that Jesus was certainly concerned with the life of man's body, with man's perishable earthly life.

Yet the human life of man's body and soul was not the only or even the main concern of Our Lord. Men already had their full human life: from the beginning God had given them complete equipment for living humanly. Those for whom our Savior worked and died had all the human life and power that was, in God's good plan, proper to them. Mankind, even after Adam's sin, was still able to live a human life. Men still had their full share of life; they still had the full power to move, grow, hear, think and love in a human way. So our dear Lord did not come to earth to give us a merely human life. We already had that. Nor did He leave Heaven to make athletes and strong men of us. He did not become man to give us clear sight, sharp hearing, strength of arm and speed of foot. Our Lord did not take flesh of Mary

8

merely to bring us learning and inventiveness or to make us mental wizards: Jesus did not walk with men merely to take away bodily troubles—weariness, sickness, worry, poverty, pain and death. No, our Savior's concern was not the human power and progress and life merely of man's body and soul.

Hence Our Lord did not give us His sacraments only to help the life of the body. Extreme Unction, if God so wills, can bring longer life to the sick body; yet that is by no means its main purpose. The priest does not recite the sacramental prayers at the bedside of the sick merely to ward off a bodily death, a death in time. The oil of Confirmation is not an ointment for external use only. The water of Baptism cleanses—but not the body. The bishop does not anoint the new priest's hands to give him bodily strength. Lastly, the sacramental Body of Christ is not eaten to take away a bodily hunger and the sacramental Blood of Christ is not consumed to quench the thirst of the body.

The most important part of man and the source, under God, of all man's human life is his soul. Yet here also we say that the first concern of our Savior, in His life and death, was not the ordinary life of man's soul. For example, our Redeemer did not urge upon men even an honest desire for money and honor and power and success. He did not preach to us a merely human devotion to country, a merely human obedience to laws. The Son of God did not want to see in us a merely human love and pity of our fellow men. Our Lord offered His own dear life for each one of us, but not to bring us a merely human clearness of thought, courage of will and

9

peace of soul. Jesus did not say, "Seek ye first for your body pleasant things—food, exercise and travel. Seek ye first for your soul a learned mind and a will devoted to your own welfare. Seek ye first to enjoy your perishable human life." But He did say: "My kingdom is not of this world." [8]

Thus it is clear that our Savior was not concerned chiefly with the perishable bodily life of His fellow men. For that matter, neither is the Catholic Church, which is Our Lord living on through the centuries of the New Testament. Let us see how in this the Catholic Church resembles Our Lord Himself. After the example of her divine Founder, the Church is indeed interested in the bodily life of mankind. Like Our Lord, the Catholic Church strives for man's bodily welfare on this earth—for example, through Catholic co-operatives, Catholic guest-houses, Catholic hospitals and Catholic schools. The Catholic Church will even pray for the temporal health and safety of men and nations. But, like our Savior again, the Church is interested in man's bodily well-being only insofar as that bodily life will help each man to save his soul. Neither did Our Lord labor nor does His Church labor merely to bring bodily comfort or health, merely to bring to man's body and soul the luxuries of this world—the telephone or the auto, electricity or radio.

But perhaps our Savior died to give each of us the glorious life of an angel. Perhaps He toiled that He might unite an angelic life to our human life of body and soul. Did Jesus in His agony and death labor to bring us

[8] John 18:36.

angelic life? No, Our Lord did not seek to lift us to the
level of the angels, lofty as that life is. The life of the
angel is far more rich and brilliant and noble than man's
human life, yet our Savior did not set His Sacred Heart
on lifting us to that glorious life. He did not labor to
give us angelic life. He did not die in order to bestow on
men angelic brilliance of mind or speed of movement.
Our Savior became man, not to make us angels, but to
make us children of God like Himself. It is true that
God gave the angels the same grace of holiness which
He bestows on us. Short of Heaven itself, this is the
greatest gift men or angels can receive from God. If men
could never deserve it, neither did the angels. It is a favor
for men; it was a favor for the angels also.

But together with this heavenly gift our Savior has
granted man gifts which even the angels never owned.
Any person with the use of reason can baptize a soul
into heavenly life, but no angel can. Any Catholic can
receive our Eucharistic God, but no angel can. A priest
can forgive sin and offer the Divine Victim at the Holy
Sacrifice, but no angel can. Our Lord raises His chosen
sons to the priesthood—a rank into which no angel has
ever entered. It does seem that Jesus in His deep love has
lifted us even beyond the life proper to the angels.

There remains only this to say. Our Lord came to give
us life, indeed, a fuller life. We have noted that our
Savior did not labor to bring us a life below our own
human life, a merely human life or even an angel's life.
Exactly what kind of life Jesus gave us, we shall now see.

CHAPTER THREE: *A Divine Life*

THE life which our Savior gives to men is a divine life. It is the gift of gifts. It is God's gift to mankind. It is God's dearest gift to us while we live on this earth.

In reality, it is sanctifying grace. It is the life of grace, the life of holiness. Spiritual writers call it our spiritual life, the life of the soul. The Catholic Church calls it our supernatural life. In her prayer [9] she refers to it as the vivifying grace, the grace that brings us to life; Pope Pius XI speaks of sanctifying grace as the permanent source of supernatural life.[10] It is the life above our human life, a higher life and a second life which God's friends live while they also lead their brief earthly life. Our Savior Himself called it a life. It is a life that can start here and go on forever in Heaven.

Always it is a life. Wherever sanctifying grace is had among us, there is found also this life. When God gives

[9] Postcommunion, Mass for the Second Sunday after Easter.
[10] Encyclical *Casti connubii*, Dec. 31, 1930.

12

a man sanctifying grace, He gives him this life. Indeed, He gives us the life which our Savior through His painful Passion sought to bring us, that is, the more abundant life.[11] In the grace called sanctifying God gives to His children the life of which we have been speaking—a divine life.

For sanctifying grace means the divine life in a man's soul. This is the wonderful fact. There is no denying it, there is no reasoning to it. It is beyond the mind of man to conceive it. No Plato could dream of it, no Edison invent it. Just as the heart of man can never conceive the glory of Heaven,[12] so neither can we picture the glory of that grace which is our passport to Heaven, sanctifying grace.

For this grace of holiness means divine life. This sanctifying grace is divine life in a person's soul. But let us go slowly now. We do not want to deceive ourselves. We must say clearly what we mean by divine life in a man's soul.

Divine life! In His own right God has it—and only God. Do we mean here that the soul in sanctifying grace has divine life as God has it? No. Do we mean that any man by receiving sanctifying grace becomes God? Impossible.

So a person with sanctifying grace does not have divine life in the way that God has it. How, then, does this grace mean divine life for mankind? In what way can we say that a man in the state of sanctifying grace has divine life? Let us see.

[11] John 10:10.
[12] I Cor. 2:9.

13

The Son of God took flesh of Mary in order to bring a fuller and richer life to mankind. That life was neither the unthinking life of the beast nor the ordinary life of man. We have noted this before. Moreover, the life Our Lord was to give us was not even the lofty life of the angels. In other words, Jesus would give to man a life above the angelic life. But there is actually only one life above that of the angels, and that is the divine life of God Himself.

If, then, Jesus gives to our human selves a life above that of the angels, it must be a life somehow divine which He gives to us. For it is a life which lifts man above all other creatures, even the angels. It is a life which lifts us, of all creatures, nearest to God. It is a life which makes a man godlike. It is a godly life. It is a life which mirrors the life of the God-man. It is a life most like God's own divine life. It is a life which is strengthened by the divine Food upon our altars. It is a life which leads us straight to eternal life with God Himself. It is a life which is in all truth a share of divine life. It is our divine life in the sense that it is a share of God's own life. That is how God Himself speaks of it. He tells us that sanctifying grace makes us "partakers of the divine nature" [13]—and therefore, we add, of the divine life.

We set out to answer a question. How does sanctifying grace in a man's soul mean divine life in that man? We shall treat this question further in a chapter entitled "Why a Divine Life?" Let it suffice now to say that sanctifying grace means divine life in a man because it

[13] II Peter 1:4.

brings him the highest life given by God to any crea-ture—the life closest to and most like God's own life, a life which is a share of God's own life.

Such is God's loving plan for mankind. Hence, as men in the state of grace walk this earth, they lead their own human lives and they live a second life too, a life nearest to the divine life of God Himself. Following God's ex-ample,[14] we call the life of sanctifying grace a share of God's own divine life. "Come and hear, all ye that fear God, and I will tell you what great things he hath done for my soul." [15]

[14] II Peter 1:4.
[15] Psalm 65:16.

CHAPTER FOUR: *Why a Life?*

Iᴛ ᴡᴀs on His Cross of pain that our Savior won the divine life of sanctifying grace for all men. God had not left Adam hopeless after his sin; for God and His Son entered into counsel, with the result that the Son of God agreed to take our flesh and die for our sins. Of course, because He was God, the Son of God would certainly carry out His pledge to the Father. He would certainly suffer and die in our place. So, with this assurance that the price of sin would be fully paid, God promised Adam a Redeemer who would raise him and his family from the deadly illness of mortal sin to the vigorous life of grace. Moreover, God immediately gave them a chance to rejoice once more in the divine life of holiness. Thus, by sorrow for their disobedience, Adam and Eve again lived the godly life of grace. Thence throughout all the centuries up to the first Good Friday, God made it possible for the human race to live the higher life of holiness. Even long before Our Lord's death for us, God was ready to share His divine life with mankind, and since that blessed moment all men have had a chance to acquire sanctifying grace and divine life. From our Savior to Peter to the Catholic Church the stream of life and grace has flowed till the present and will flow unto the end of time. As we glow with the godly life of sanctifying grace, let us thank Him who saved our divine life for us—Jesus, our Life-Giver.

But now we have a question about our divine life. This life is in reality a gift of God called sanctifying grace. This is the grace that sanctifies, that makes us saintly or holy. Sanctifying grace is holiness itself. It is placed within our soul by God and we become holy by its presence within us. In fact, sanctifying grace is the only thing that really makes us holy. Hence without it we are unholy in God's sight, and with it we are holy, we are saints of God.

So sanctifying grace is holiness itself. Yet all along we have said that it is life—our second life, our higher life, our divine life. How can that be? How can sanctifying grace be both our holiness and our life? For, of themselves, holiness and life are not one and the same thing. Indeed, it is a sad truth that human life and holiness do not always go together. Many a sinner is full of life but at the same time he is an unholy man.

How then is this one thing, sanctifying grace, both holiness and life? Clearly sanctifying grace is holiness, for it is the very thing that gives holiness, that makes us holy. But how is it also life? What right have we to say that sanctifying grace is life?

We can say that sanctifying grace is life because God

tells us so in His own words. In Sacred Scripture [16] we read that those who receive Our Lord "are born not of blood nor of the will of the flesh nor of the will of man but of God." Those who receive our Savior are they who "believe in his name" and share in His grace—the sanctifying grace of holiness. Clearly such believers already have their complete human life, the life with which they were born into the world. Yet God tells us that these believers are "born of God." Furthermore, God shows us in three different ways that He is not speaking of human birth. It is not a question of passing on the family blood ("not of blood"), of being born of fleshly selfishness ("nor of the will of the flesh"), or of being born of a fatherly desire ("nor of the will of man"). But those believers who have the sanctifying grace of holiness are "born of God." The holy are born of God. Now those who are born receive a life like that of their father. So those who are "born of God" receive a life like God's own life, a godly life, a life somehow divine. Hence the holy, those born of God, receive a life from God, a godlike divine life.

At this point let us stop for a moment. We have just noted a wonderful fact. The holy are born of God. By his birth from God the holy man receives a life. The holy man lives the human life he received from his mother and father but he lives also the new and divine life he has received from being born of God. Here then is the answer to our question: How is the one thing—that is, sanctifying grace—both our holiness and our life? Sanctifying grace is our holiness because it is the precise

[16] John 1:12–13.

thing that makes a man holy. Sanctifying grace is our life because those who have it are "born of God," that is, they receive from God and live a life, a true life and a new life. Through sanctifying grace man is both holy and alive with a higher life. In this way the one thing, sanctifying grace, is both our holiness and our life. In this way too, our holiness means and is our life, indeed a life born of God Himself.

Our divine life is begotten of God. It is beyond our ideas of human greatness. It is beyond our mind to conceive of it. Only God could so plan that our being holy means living with a new and second life. Then God told us of our added life in His own words: the holy are "born of God." By that birth from God saintly souls live in the intimacy of a true and higher life. Let us work all our days to live in that same divine intimacy.

Man, by becoming holy, is born of God and begins to live a second and new and higher life. God Himself told us this in very plain words. Jesus, the Son of God, also brings us this same joyful message. The living God had decreed that the grace of holiness in our souls is a living holiness, a divinely begotten life.

In the Gospel [17] our Savior is speaking to Nicodemus, a Pharisee. At the time the Jews felt that the birth of the Messias was near. Moreover, Nicodemus was forced to think along these lines when he saw the wonders that Jesus wrought. Thus we find him coming to our Savior with some thought that He might be the Messias.

Nicodemus believes that, because he is of the race of Abraham, he will surely enter Heaven. Jesus tells him

[17] John 3:1 ff.

about the new law of holiness and salvation: "Unless a man be born again, he cannot see the kingdom of God." To Nicodemus this is a new doctrine which he does not understand. He knows only one kind of birth for men, as his question shows. "How can a man be born when he is old? Can he enter a second time into his mother's womb and be born again?" Nicodemus is thinking of the birth by which every man is born into this world. Jesus is not speaking of this birth from woman. He is talking about being born "again." And who are sure to be born "again"? Those who would see the kingdom of God are to be born again, that is, those who would enter Heaven. Now from the beginning of the human race to the Last Judgment, no man can enter Heaven without sanctifying grace. This grace alone is the key to our eternal happiness. It is the only possession our soul needs when God calls us out of this world. Hence this is what our Savior is teaching us: they are to be born again who would enter Heaven. They are born a second time who possess the grace of holiness. Sanctifying grace within us is a second birth, a second life.

But because Nicodemus does not grasp this glorious truth, Jesus repeats it. "Amen, amen I say to thee, unless a man be born again of water and the Holy Ghost, he cannot enter into the kingdom of God." Those who would "enter into the kingdom of God" must "be born again of water and the Holy Ghost." In Our Lord's religion no one can enter Heaven without being born again in the sacrament of Baptism. That is the ordinary law of Christ's Church. So those who have sanctifying grace have been "born again of water and the Holy Ghost."

After Baptism man continues to live his human life; but with Baptism he has been born "again." He has received a second life, a new life. The baptized man now leads two lives, a life begotten of his parents and a life begotten of God. Thus does our Savior teach us that by Baptism we receive the grace of holiness and a new rich life. Our holiness means and is our second life. "Wonder not that I said to thee, you must be born again." [18]

God tells us holy souls are "born of God." [19] Moreover, He tells us that the life of holiness is not a life born of the flesh; it is a life begotten of God. Then in His own words to Nicodemus Our Lord preaches the same glorious message. For He shows us clearly that souls baptized unto holiness are born "again" of the Holy Ghost. These are not only born once but they are begotten a second time. In this way they receive a second and new life. After Baptism has given the soul sanctifying grace, that soul is holy in itself and alive with a second life. Our holiness is our life.

But, because this truth is so important, God has revealed it in other parts of Sacred Scripture, namely, through the First Epistle of St. Peter and the epistles of St. Paul. The latter writes that, when our Savior appeared, "He saved us by the laver of regeneration and renovation of the Holy Ghost." [20] Our Lord saves us through the laver, that is, through the water of Baptism, because Baptism washes original sin from our souls, brings sanctifying grace into our souls and puts man on

[18] John 3:7.
[19] John 1:13.
[20] Titus 3:5.

the direct road to Heaven. For that is the work of Baptism in Christ's Church. This work St. Paul explains by the words "the laver of regeneration." Baptism cleanses, sanctifies and at the same time regenerates the soul. Hence it implies a second birth added to the first birth, a second life added to the first life. So sanctifying grace in the soul of a newly baptized person means a second birth for that person, a second life.

Lastly, St. Peter writes concerning our redemption by Our Lord: "Jesus Christ . . . hath regenerated us unto a lively hope." [21] Again it is a question of regeneration. Through the grace won for us by our Savior we are regenerated. Souls with the grace of holiness are born again and live a second life. For us holiness will always mean a new true life in Christ Jesus.

In this chapter and in the preceding chapter we have seen five texts of Scripture. In these five places God has revealed to us a truth we could never know of ourselves. On God's word five times spoken to us we believe this ennobling truth: that the holy soul is alive with a second and a rich life. We can, in fact, have no holiness that is not a living holiness. The holy man is alive with two lives, his life of body and soul plus his life begotten of God. To be holy is to be alive as one born even of God Himself.

Thus we have learned that the sanctifying grace of God means both our holiness and our life. It is a truth that urges us on to greater virtue and a more godlike life, a life somehow divine. We may say that it is not for us. We may say that such a life is for God's saints only.

[21] I Peter 1:3.

The Life That Is Grace

But you are God's saints! For you are in the state of grace. You are living a life beyond that of food and drink. You are aglow with a second life, you are alive with a richer life than that of body and soul. God has revealed this to you. Be sure that you have within yourselves this second life, the life of the soul. "Wonder not that I said to thee, you must be born again." [22]

[22] John 3:7.

CHAPTER FIVE: *Why a Divine Life?*

Sᴏᴍᴇᴛɪᴍᴇs a person is called a man of the world. He is one who knows the things of the world. He is aware of the news behind the news. He dines well. He reads the newest magazines. He follows the sport page in the daily papers. His talk flows along the lines of the day's thought, so often godless. His life is concerned only with the theatre, fashions, the table, conversation, reading and, in general, pleasure.

The man of the world knows hardly anything of another world about him—another world of living men, of men alive with a second and a higher life. A man living with this life is a man of God. Unlike the man of the world, the man of God is not concerned only with pleasure and worldly things. The man of God is a holy person. His clothes may never be smart; he may never dine well; he need never read the newest novels; he may be ignorant of modern thought. Yet if he has the grace

24

of holiness within his soul, such a one is a man of God. He is a man of God because he is holy and, as holy, he is one born of God. He is a man of God because through sanctifying grace he is born again of God. He is of God because his soul is alive with a second life begotten of God.

Now, that second life is a life somehow divine. In the last two chapters we stressed the fact that sanctifying grace gave us another life and a true life. Here we want to show that this second life, this life of holiness, is a life somehow divine. Our grace-life is a life entirely beyond the merely human or angelic, a life on the divine level, a life like that proper to God Himself.

We saw already that holy people are "born of God";[23] we noted too that baptized men are born again "of the Holy Ghost." [24] Let us look carefully at those words, "of God" and "of the Holy Ghost." For when among creatures living things are born, they receive a life like that of their parents. Indeed, this is what men mean by birth. So, when holy people are born of God, they receive a life like God's own life. When baptized souls are born of the Holy Ghost, they must receive a life somehow divine. In our baptismal birth the Father grafts a new and higher life on our human life, begets a new and divine life within our soul. The living supernatural grace of God is welded to our soul, the divine to the human. In Baptism the soul is transformed into a richer likeness of God, for whom to live is always to be holy; in the newly born child of God the divine life thence-

[23] John 1:13.
[24] John 3:5.

forth will also demand holiness. Thus on God's word that we are born of Himself, we say our second life is a divine life.

We believe, then, that the grace of holiness gives us a godlike life. It is not a life we can see or touch, but it is all the more godlike for that. Of course, it is partly a mystery. God has told us this truth and so we are certain of it. We believe it with all our mind and shall try to live our godly life. But even after God has revealed to us the fact of our godlike life, we do not fully understand it. That is why we say our life of holiness is a life "somehow" divine; that is why we say the divine life within us is a mystery.

Yet we can, to some extent, know and appreciate the godlike life within us. The Jews of the Old Testament were sure they would enter Heaven because they had received their human life from the seed of Abraham. They were of the race chosen by God. However, Our Lord told them that in His religion holiness and Heaven did not depend on one's being born into human life from some special seed or blood or father or race. In the New Testament no man can be holy or be saved unless through Baptism he is born again of the Holy Ghost. Our holiness is a birth into a life somehow divine; and so it is no human blood or life but that divine life of grace which makes men holy and allows men to enter Heaven. In this way our Savior teaches us that the life of holiness within us is, by His grace, a divine life begotten of God.

We are born of God. So God Himself says, and we are happy to take Him at His word. Born of God! The

Lord God begot His Son, the Second Person of the Blessed Trinity. In the Creed recited at Mass the priest says of God the Son that He was "born, not made"; we can say the same of holy souls in their divine life. For God begets them through the grace of holiness. Except for His Son, men and angels are the only ones born of God. The rocks and the sea were made by God. The flowers and the beasts were made by God. They are not born of God. Even our human bodies are made by God. Then our souls are created by God. Of all the creatures we know, it is to men and angels alone that the grace of divine life has been given. Other things may be the products of God's power but holy men are God's off-spring. Even our human life of body and soul is made by God; but for us to live the godly life of holiness, we must be born of God.

Of course, God could have granted us our grace-life without regenerating us. He could simply have produced it as He did the new life of body and soul for Adam. But he deigned to beget man's grace-life of Himself, so that man with sanctifying grace is not merely His handiwork but His child born of Himself. God does not merely make us holy; He begets us to holiness. Our holiness, therefore, is a life and a divine life. That is why we are living two lives, a human life and a godly life. That is why we are born to holiness.

Sanctifying grace is the fruit of the sacraments. Speaking of these holy rites, Pope Pius XII calls them "rivers of divine grace and divine life." [25] Our Pontiff tells us that our grace-life is a "divine life." Indeed, the tiniest

[25] Encyclical *Mediator Dei*, Nov. 20, 1947.

share of sanctifying grace which man possesses—for instance, the first unit of grace given the infant at Baptism—means he is living the divine life. Just as the littlest babe is truly a man, so the baptized child with the first gift of grace flooding his soul is truly alive with the divine life.

God has revealed all this to us. He has made the process by which we are sanctified through Baptism a process also of birth. God has lifted our holiness to so high a plane that it is a divinely living holiness. The gift of God within us, sanctifying grace, is so much above our human way of life that a man, in order to possess it, must be begotten of the living God.

Thus we come to our conclusion. Since it is God of whom we have been born through Baptism, our life of holiness can rightly be called a divine life.

CHAPTER SIX: *Where Is This Life?*

I

WHEN by God's grace a man is made holy, there dwells within his soul a divine life. This is no mere case of "as if" or "let us suppose." For the higher life of man is as real as his own soul; indeed, the life of grace is a greater and nobler part of a holy person than even the soul itself. For example, when Adam's body received his soul, it took on a human life; but when his soul received sanctifying grace, that soul began to live a life higher than the human. A life somehow divine filled Adam's soul; it flowed over into the powers of his soul, into his mind and will; it entered into his soul's every deed— thoughts and desires and love. Such is, in truth, the picture of a holy soul, suffused as it is with divine life.

Thus, within the body, the soul and sanctifying grace live together. God has given us both of them; God has joined both in closest union. Together they dwell, the human soul and divine grace; and together they will work all our years to bring us into Heaven. Yes, even when in death the soul leaves the body, even then divine life still floods our soul and goes together with it to unending joy. That indeed will be the happy hour in which death finds our soul embracing forever the divine life of grace!

Hence, as long as we have sanctifying grace, it is our soul that possesses it. That is why a person can say: "I enjoy the divine life of grace." What such a one means is: "Mine is the soul to which God has joined His grace. So mine is the divine life that grace gives." It is a man's soul which lives the divine life of grace; then through his soul he personally enjoys that divine life.

Moreover, it is quite understandable that, if once God should ever decide to give us the life of grace, He would place that life within man's soul. For the life of sanctifying grace is not a thing to be measured by any yardstick or timepiece; but in this it is like God's own life, that it is spiritual and is intended to go on eternally. So we shall look for the life of grace in man's spiritual and ever-living part, in man's finest part—that is, his soul; and there we shall find it. Joined together in closest union are the soul and sanctifying grace, human life and divine life! Embraced in holiest love are the spiritual soul and the spiritual life of grace, the soul that will live eternally and the life of grace that can go on forever! In other words, a holy person lives the divine life because he has a soul which can receive the full force of sanctifying grace. That is why it is our soul which enjoys the divine life.

It will now be helpful to see what follows from this happy fact. The part of man which God has begotten unto the divine life of grace is his soul. On the one hand, sanctifying grace needs that soul as a dwelling-place which it can make holy; on the other hand, it is our soul's glory to receive sanctifying grace, to have God's grace penetrate its every part, its inmost self and its powers. It is our soul's privilege to let the grace of holiness enliven it with a new and divine life.

This is a sight that always gladdens the angels and the blessed in Heaven. For this is what we mean by the one important word "salvation." From earliest childhood every Catholic hears this word and learns its meaning as the life of grace within his soul. Ezechiel [26] puts it thus: "He shall save his soul alive." The giving of this divine life to the souls of men is the work of the Catholic Church through its prayers, the Holy Sacrifice and the sacraments. For instance, in giving Holy Communion the priest prays: "May the Body of Our Lord Jesus Christ guard your soul unto life everlasting." At the moment of death it is the soul that is of chief concern to priest and people. Hence we ask God's mercy in this way: "May his soul and the souls of all the faithful departed rest in peace." Again, when the saints cried out to God for souls, they wanted God to help them win souls to the divine life of grace—and thereby to holiness and salvation, to the Catholic Church and Heaven.

Lastly, we shall speak about Our Lord. He was given the sacred name of Jesus, showing that He came to save mankind: "Thou shalt call his name Jesus. For he shall save his people from their sins." [27] He was always our

26 Ezech. 18:27.
27 Matt. 1:21.

Savior; all His life He labored to save souls. Moreover, He taught us the value of a man's soul. It is more important than the world; we must ever be ready to give up the whole world if that is needed in order to save a soul. "For what doth it profit a man if he gain the whole world and suffer the loss of his own soul? Or what shall a man give in exchange for his soul?" [28] Indeed, we must sacrifice life itself and prefer even death when that is the price of our salvation. "And fear ye not them that kill the body and are not able to kill the soul." [29]

Jesus climaxed His life as our Savior by His death on Calvary. He chose that death in order thereby to give us sanctifying grace, the soul's divine life. His sufferings measure the value He placed on a man's soul; they are the price He paid in exchange for our souls. When we call Jesus our life-giver and our Savior, we mean with all reverence that He is our lifesaver, the saver of our richer, fuller life. The more abundant life which Our Lord always gives to His friends is the divine life of grace within our souls.

II

We have seen that our higher life comes to us through sanctifying grace. So we will find this life wherever sanctifying grace is had. That grace is in our soul; and hence it is there that we possess our precious life of holiness.

Thus our divine life is not something outside ourselves. It is not something that can be carried in a purse or brief

[28] Matt. 16:26.
[29] Matt. 10:28.

case. For our godly life is within our very soul. It is inside us, in the most intimate and important part of our selves. The life of grace abides deep within man's own nature. Our supernatural life is in the very essence and being of our soul.

Here it may be useful to note a point. The divine life and man's soul are certainly two different things. Indeed, they need not be found together at all as, for instance, in the unbaptized soul. But as long as we are friends of God, our souls possess the divine life of grace. Moreover, this life is not merely within the soul as something separate from it, like a trinket in a boy's pocket. Grace and the soul are not two objects that come close together but never touch one another. The truth is that our soul and our divine life are united most closely to each other. Our higher life is wedded to, grafted on, fused into the soul. As soul joins the body to give that body human life, so grace joins the soul to give that soul divine life. Not only is the life of grace within the soul but it permeates the soul. Together sanctifying grace and the soul are united in the closest union of love and life.

In this way our soul enjoys divine life. For it is our soul that has received sanctifying grace; it is our soul that has been born again of God unto a life divine. Our soul, already living its human life, is through sanctifying grace alive with a second life. That is why God's grace is called the life of the soul. Indeed, so true is this that a soul which has never received sanctifying grace is a soul without divine life, even though it possess its full human life.

Of course, the divine life within us is not a life that can be seen or heard or touched. It is a life above the world of size and weight, measure and money. It is a spiritual life, like God's own divine life. It is a life hidden from men, though not from God: "Your life is hid with Christ in God." [30] As living flesh is grafted on other living flesh till both grow together in one life, so is the divine life of grace grafted on the living soul by God. Thus does the soul acquire its divine life.

Furthermore, we know that the soul extends itself throughout our body. Whether a man is large or small, there is no living part of his flesh where the soul does not abide. We now want to say the same thing about our divine life. The soul is found throughout the entire body; the life of grace is found throughout the whole soul. Hence all who are God's friends can point to any part of their flesh and say: "Because my soul is here, so too is my divine life." Our soul extends to the full depth and breadth of our flesh. In like manner our divine life, always remaining in the soul, extends itself to every spot in our body. Remember those words: "Always remaining in the soul."

In this way man's body is ennobled as the home of the soul's divine life. Our body becomes a temple, housing the fuller life of sanctifying grace. Thus, even the bodies of God's holy ones grow in honor and dignity; and this thought may well deter those who would cheapen the body or use it only for the body's sake. Yet while the body houses sanctifying grace, it is the soul alone that is

[30] Col. 3:3.

united in life and love to God's grace. Only our soul possesses the more abundant life; only our soul is lifted above itself to the higher life; only our soul is flooded with the divine life of grace and holiness.

CHAPTER SEVEN: *The Common Voca-*
tion of All Men

O UR divine life, glorious though it be, is not destined
only for special souls. For where our birth into the
divine life is concerned, God calls all men. Hence this
call is not merely for presidents and kings; it is not for
priests or religious only; neither does one receive the call
just by being mighty or rich or cultured; nor is it only
for some chosen race or privileged class of men. Rather,
God wished the divine life of grace to be lived by every
man born of Adam. This vocation is a free call from
God, free on His part and undeserved on ours. "You
have not chosen me but I have chosen you." [31]

It need not surprise us that the whole of mankind is
called to the divine life. For, as in God's plan all men
derive the one human life from our father Adam, so likewise God planned that the divine life of holiness should
be the common life of mankind. Had Adam obeyed
God, this divine life would have been the birthright of

[31] John 15:16.

the human race. Furthermore, because Jesus on His Cross redeemed us, the divine life of grace is still the common destiny of our human race. For now we live in the New Testament of our Savior and it is the glory of His Testament to be catholic—that is, for *all* men until the end of time. Christ and His Apostles preached the Gospel "to the Jew first," [32] but He and they always made it clear that the call to divine life and holiness and Christianity was not for the chosen people only but for all men of all future ages. St. Paul taught that Jew and Gentile are both destined for grace and holiness: "Even us, whom also he hath called, not only of the Jews but also of the Gentiles." [33] In this way the Catholic Church has, since her first day, obeyed the commands of her Founder: "Go ye into the whole world and preach the gospel to every creature." [34] For from Him the Church has learned that the call to divine life is for the entire human race—men and women, young and old, down to the tiniest baby.

What then do we mean by saying that all men are called to the divine life? Certainly God gives to every man by birth a life of flesh and blood; but in regard to the divine life of holiness God acts differently. Because this life of sanctifying grace is divine, man needs help from God in order to receive it. This help, while always of a divine order, will differ for different souls. It may be the charity or the beauty or the rites of the Catholic Church which will lead men to inquire into the truth of

[32] Rom. 1:16.
[33] Rom. 9:24.
[34] Mark 16:15.

that Church; it may be the holy example of a Catholic or the advice of a priest which will draw men to follow Christ. Certainly required in order to bring the divine life to souls are God's actual graces and the sacrament of Baptism. But, whatever help is needed, God gives every soul a chance to use it and to profit by it, so that he may receive the divine life of grace. In this way does God call all men to the divine life.

Thus every soul has a vocation to the divine life. Hence it is wrong to say that lay people are not called to live the divine life—indeed, to grow in it. For this life of grace is the vocation of married and single, religious and priest. Only too well do we see that God invites all souls to the heavenly life of holiness, when we notice how each walk of life has its saints. There are saints of the cloister, the world, the kitchen and the throne, the classroom and the farm, the factory and the law courts. Certain souls, by sacrificing the world and entering into the cloister, have better ways of growing in the divine life; nevertheless, it is the same divine life of sanctifying grace to which God calls all men from infancy to old age, from one century to another. "Among whom are you also, the called of Jesus Christ . . . the beloved of God, called to be saints." [35] The vocations to marriage and the single life, to the priesthood and the religious life are really special vocations within this general vocation of mankind. Thus, no matter what each one is personally, he has the God-given vocation of living the divine life.

Yes, and he has received also a God-given duty. We

[35] Rom. 1:6–7.

know that, in God's plan, one law and purpose of life is to pass itself on to future generations; if this were not so, all life would die out. In regard to human life, only they have the duty of continuing our bodily life who are truly married. Concerning the divine life, we say that all men are called to pass it on. Of course this is especially true of those who enjoy the life of grace themselves. And how can they pass on the supernatural life to their spiritual descendants? They do this by personal dealing with their neighbors, by holy example, by the heavenly value of their good deeds, and by the sacraments (for example, by baptizing other souls). Thus they bring the divine life to those who have not been born of God and they help raise sinners from the deathbed of mortal sin to the healthy life of sanctifying grace. This same mission of begetting souls unto the divine life is also the duty of the Catholic Church. For the Church is the Body of Christ; and as it was His task to be the Savior of divine life for all men, so too is His Church called to prevent soul-death and to pass on to her children the Christ-life itself. For this divine purpose does the Church send every Catholic as a missionary into the world, that the children of men may be born into the divine childhood. When there is danger of death, the Catholic Church will even seek to baptize the infant in the womb and thus bring forth another child of God. With full right do we call our Church "Holy Mother the Church."

Here let us note a likeness between the human life of man and his divine life. Certainly a person must first receive the life of flesh and blood from his parents before he can receive the divine life of grace—but to both lives God calls all mankind. Furthermore, God wants men to help Him pass on both the human and the divine lives. In God's plan marriage is the way in which men work with Him to produce human life, while it is in Baptism that God and man co-operate to beget souls unto the divine life.

However, husband and wife often forget that God wishes them through their union to pass on their own bodily life to their children. "And God blessed them saying: Increase and multiply and fill the earth." [36] So also do even Catholics forget that it is their duty as apostles to help God spread the divine life. How beautiful are the fruits of man's labor in union with God! Husband, wife and God—each has a part to play in the loving trinity of marriage. While husband and wife work together to form an infant body, God creates a human soul; and the fruit of the loving union between man and God is a new human life. In like manner do Catholic lay apostles, foreign missionaries, priests and the Catholic Church work with God in their vocation to beget divine life, and as the fruit of this union there is born to God the Father a man's soul—alive with the divine life of sanctifying grace.

Such then is the divine life into which God invites all men to be born. Such too is the life of holiness which it is our duty to generate in other souls. Called to live the divine life ourselves, we are likewise called to father it in our spiritual descendants. In this we follow our Savior

[36] Gen. 1:28.

Himself, whose glory it is both to live the divine life and to share it with His fellow men.

Our vocation to the divine life is a God-given call, a sacred cause to which we must dedicate ourselves. We must gladly fulfill the duties of this holy call. In our Catholic life we must bear in mind constantly that holiness is our vocation—the highest holiness we can, with God's grace, attain. That is our supernatural destiny in Christ and in God. St. Paul calls his fellow Christians "holy brethren, partakers of the heavenly vocation"; [37] we, with our call to the divine life of grace, are also "holy brethren, partakers of the heavenly vocation."

[37] Heb. 3:1.

CHAPTER EIGHT: *A Twice-given Life*

In the beginning God made man. He took the dust of the earth and breathed into it a living, life-giving soul. That soul united with the dust to form the first living man. Then God added to Adam's soul the greatest gift of all, sanctifying grace. It was a gift undeserved on Adam's part. It was an outright gift of God. It was a gift of heavenly holiness. It was especially a living, life-giving gift. Adam already had a perfect human life of body and soul. Now sanctifying grace gave him a higher life, a share of God's own divine life.

Thus Adam stood before God in Paradise. As his soul had lifted the dust of the earth into a living human being, so sanctifying grace lifted man into a being with a higher life. As Adam's soul had given him a perfect human life, so sanctifying grace gave Adam a share of the divine life.

From earth to man—what a leap! From no life to life, from the lifeless dust to a seeing, knowing, loving man—what a change! Compare yourself with the dust under

your feet, with the earth in the wheels of your automobile, with the dust clinging to your shoes—only God
could lift that clod of dirt into a reasoning man! Yet a
still greater change was wrought when God placed
sanctifying grace in Adam's soul. To make man, God
breathed a soul into the dead dust; then the Spirit of God
breathed divine life into frail man. For the grace of holiness in Adam's soul gave him a superhuman life, a godlike life.

This was the first time that human life dwelt on the
earth; and that was wonderful enough. But this was the
first time too that a man had received sanctifying grace
and, with it, a life above his own human life. God had
shared His divine life with a man, a creature He had
made from nothing. Yet God was not satisfied with even
this bounteous favor to the first man, for He wanted all
the children of Adam to live the divine life of sanctifying grace. So in His wisdom He made Adam the care-
taker of his children's heavenly life.

This was the plan. Adam would be the father of all
men. Through generation he would pass on to each of
his children a complete, perfect human life. God would
not make our human life, as a race, depend on someone
else's conduct—our sight and hearing, our power to walk
and talk and think. If God would put man into this
world, we could expect to have a perfect human life of
body and soul. But we had no claim at all to the second
and higher life of sanctifying grace. So God could and
did make our receiving of divine life depend on Adam's
obedience. If Adam disobeyed God, each child would be
born into only human life. If Adam obeyed, his children

43

would be born to lead two lives—their own human life plus the divine life of sanctifying grace.

Adam, however, disobeyed God. His sin was deadly; and so he lost the divine life of sanctifying grace for himself and for us. Adam was still alive as a man. He could move, speak, eat, think, love and have children. He could do the things of a man. He was still a complete man. But he and Eve were no longer alive with the divine life of grace. They lived only one life, their own human life. Moreover, their children would be born like themselves —that is, with human life, but dead to the life of grace. Their children had lost the chance of entering into the world alive with a second and higher life. The human race had been deprived of its greatest gift.

It was the first crisis that had arisen for mankind and it was the worst that would ever arise. Adam and Eve were no longer godlike; and the whole race, billions of men, would no longer be godly. Before God, man was dead; and, as dead, he could of course never help himself to live again with divine life. With the exception of Our Lord, dead men do not raise themselves to life again. God alone gave Adam the first grace that lifted man to a divine level of life; God alone could again raise man from the dead to the divine life of grace. Only God's boundless love had moved Him to lift man to a divine intimacy; only that same limitless love could again stir Him to share His divine life with mankind. Would it so stir Him? It would. "By this hath the charity of God appeared towards us, because God hath sent his only begotten Son into the world that we may live by him." [38]

[38] I John 4:9.

So for the second time the divine life of sanctifying grace was offered to mankind. The crisis had passed.

This was the new plan. To make up for the insult of Adam's sin God demanded a full return of love and honor. Only thus would He again give man the higher life of grace. But clearly no man, and especially the race dead in God's sight, could ever give God this full measure of love and honor. So God, who "hath first loved us," [39] commanded His Son to take on our human flesh, to suffer and die in that human life and thus make full payment for Adam's deadly sin. In this way God's justice would be satisfied and the children of Adam would once again be able to live the life of grace. The plan worked perfectly. The Son of God willed to obey His Father's command: "As the Father hath given me commandment, so do I." [40]

Then, at the chosen moment, God's Son took flesh of Mary and became Jesus Christ, our Savior. "But when the fulness of the time was come, God sent his Son, made of a woman." [41] Our Lord's whole life was pleasing to His Father but it was especially His Passion and death that the Father demanded as the payment for the insult of sin and as the means of winning sanctifying grace for men. Lovingly Jesus suffered and died for His fellow men. He "loved me and delivered himself for me." [42] By His bloody death Our Lord paid the price of sin and also won for us the divine life of sanctifying grace. As sin and death came to us from Adam, so grace and life have

[39] I John 4:10.
[40] John 14:31.
[41] Gal. 4:4.
[42] Gal. 2:20.

come to us through our Savior. How fitting it is that He who is also God should lay down His human life in order to give men a share of His divine life! Our Lord laid down the life He had in common with us in order to give us a share of the life He had in common with His Father. It was again possible for the children of Adam to be alive with the divine life of sanctifying grace.

In fact, the divine life restored to mankind by our Savior is richer than the grace-life lost by Adam in the beginning of the race. True, Adam enjoyed and we enjoy sanctifying grace, the very heart of our divine life; yet we, through Christ, are endowed with supernatural gifts above Adam's. We live in the New Testament, which is the completing and perfecting of the Old Testament. We dwell in the Church Christ founded, as members of His Mystical Body. Therein the teachings of Jesus guide us, the example of Jesus inspires us, the life of Jesus enlivens us. Under Christ we have the sacraments as the source of divine grace and life and growth. We offer the one true Sacrifice most pleasing to God because in it we offer the God-man to the Father. Holy Communion is the truly divine Food, nourishing our life of holiness. In the Catholic Church we are children of the divine family—with Mary as our Mother, Jesus as our Brother and God as our Father.

Such is the history of sanctifying grace and our higher life. Plainly this life of holiness is a twice-given gift of God. It is the most valuable gift we have, because it cost the precious life of our Savior. It is the most important gift we have, because without it we can never gain our eternal happiness. When we consider the value and importance of this divine life, we can well give thanks to God for His generous love in giving us twice the godly life of sanctifying grace.

CHAPTER NINE: *A New Life*

THE baptism of an infant and the forgiveness of a sinner are events most pleasing to God; for both infant and sinner receive the grace of holiness, sanctifying grace—and what a change that makes in men!

A moment before the priest says "I baptize you" and "I absolve you," we are our complete human selves. We live the life of body and soul. But when we have been baptized and absolved, we have body and soul plus God's abiding grace. This gift, coming into the soul, floods soul and body with a higher life. As the soul gives the whole body its human life, so sanctifying grace gives man's body and soul a divine life. A moment ago man's whole being was alive with its proper human life; now that whole being surges with a new and divine life also. Furthermore, the soul, enlivened by sanctifying grace, penetrates every part of the body and hence the grace of divine life is carried throughout one's entire being. In fact, St. Thomas Aquinas [43] tells us that, while sanctifying grace properly dwells in the soul, its holy influence helps the body too. So is the whole man renewed by the grace of holiness.

By the grace of sanctity a person becomes a wholly new man. A new life floods his entire being. A person may, after God's grace has entered into him, seem to be the same as he was before—but he is not the same. He is no longer a mere man; he is a man who is godlike. The new gift of grace has renovated his soul; it has made his soul new in God's sight. The infant just baptized and the sinner just forgiven glow with a new life fresh from God, a never-failing life from the never-failing source of life. They are new men, entirely alive with a new life.

This change worked in us by sanctifying grace is noted by St. Paul when he speaks of the old man and the new man: "Put off . . . the old man . . . And put on the new man." [44] Who is the old man and who is the new? St. Paul tells us who these men are. Our "old man" is "the body of sin," [45] that is, our human self subject to sin. Our "old man . . . is corrupted according to the desire of error." [46] On the other hand, "the new man" is he "who according to God is created in justice and holiness of truth." [47] It is clear, then, what it means for us to put off the old man and put on the new. We must pass from our old life of sin to the new life of "justice and holiness," that is, sanctifying grace. Our former sinful

[43] *Summa Theologica*, Part III, q. 79, art. 1, *ad* 3.
[44] Eph. 4:22, 24.
[45] Rom. 6:6.
[46] Eph. 4:22.
[47] Eph. 4:24.

self has ceased to be; another self has come to live in us. Our old self, dying in sin, was on the road to the eternal death of hell; our new self, living in grace, is on the road to the eternal life of Heaven.

By birth a new nature comes to life; the grace given through Baptism is a new nature in God's new child. Just as Simon became Peter and Levi became Matthew in their new life as Apostles, so we in Baptism receive the name of a saint to show that now we are new men with a new Christian life. In sanctifying grace our human nature takes on a new and higher nature with the power to live and act in a new and higher way worthy of Heaven. The virtue of faith gives us a "newness of . . . mind"; [48] the virtues of hope and charity give us new wills turned to God. In the sanctified soul the Blessed Trinity takes up a new and loving presence. Thus sanctifying grace renews every aspect of our human life—our mind and will and nature. Through it, moreover, we have been received into a new family—God's. We have Jesus for a Brother, the Holy Spirit as our Guest, Mary as our Mother, and the saints on earth as fellow members of our divine family.

Thus the man who is sanctified by grace is an entirely new kind of being. He has taken on a "newness of spirit" [49] and a "newness of life." [50] His whole self is alive with a new and divine life. On God's part, he is a new creation, "created in justice and holiness." He is a "new creature." [51] He has put off his old Adam of sin

[48] Rom. 12:2.
[49] Rom. 7:6.
[50] Rom. 6:4.
[51] II Cor. 5:17.

and now enjoys the fresh divine life of the newly created Adam in Paradise. Indeed, it is only this life of grace which makes our own earth a paradise!

But there is another way in which the life of holiness is new. It is different from every other life on earth; it is different from the human life which came to us through our parents. Moreover, it is not just *more* of that same life. In fact, there is nothing else on earth exactly like our new life of grace, for this life which holy people possess is above all other created life. Not only does man by grace rise above himself but he is lifted above the angelic nature also. Let us recall here that our holiness comes to us through a birth. Now birth, whether from man or God, means always a new life. That is why sanctifying grace gives us a new living nature. Furthermore, in our Baptism, it is of God that we are born; and so our second life is a life like our new Parent's, a life somehow divine. It is a life in the image of God's life—"putting on the new, him who is renewed unto knowledge, according to the image of him that created him." [52] The new life within our being is like only unto God's life: "Put on the new man who according to God is created in justice and holiness of truth." [53] Note St. Paul's words: "according to the image of him that created him" and "according to God." The living God Himself is the model for our life of grace. Our new life is godlike; as new men, we live a divine life. Then, once we possess the grace-life, we can by our virtuous deeds advance to newer degrees of holiness—thus becoming less worldly, more saintly,

[52] Col. 3:10.
[53] Eph. 4:24.

more Catholic, more divinely alive. The diamond under the play of light gives off new color and beauty and brilliance; every grace we use will bring out newer growth and virtue and beauty in our life of sanctity.

Hence we can well call our life of grace the very highest created life. Hence too does it cause the greatest change in men. The change from the graceless soul to the soul newly living the divine life is more wondrous than the creation of the universe by God, more stupendous than Christ's raising the dead to life. The change wrought in us by sanctifying grace is greater than the change from unmarried to married, blind to seeing, unschooled to learned, poor to rich, sick to healthy. For the grace that is life changes us from worldly to heavenly, from ungodly to godlike, from sinners to saints, from children of men to children of God. And this wonder of God's grace happens daily all over the world!

An example of what the new life of grace can do in a willing soul is Matt Talbot, the Irish workingman. On a late afternoon, Matt, out of work, stood on a corner where his friends of the lumberyard would pass. These same men he had often treated. Now Matt wanted a drink—but in vain. Hurt by the thanklessness of his comrades, he returned home, where his mother served him dinner. Then he went to church, made his first confession in three years and took the pledge. The new life of grace flooded Matt's whole being and Matt helped that life to run its full course. He never again drank liquor; he prayed long; he helped the foreign missions out of his small pay; he did great penance; he was at his daily work in the lumberyard; the church became his home morning and evening; and in 1925 he died on the very steps of the church. Such is the change that took place in Matt Talbot after Penance restored to him the full life of sanctifying grace. For fifteen years before his confession he had been lost to drink; during the rest of his days he was a holy son of God, a new man living the new life of sanctifying grace.

So too should all men be who have been born to the divine life. For theirs is a new holiness and a holy newness. St. Paul reminds us of our Savior's resurrection from the tomb: "That as Christ is risen from the dead . . . so we also may walk in newness of life." [54] The person who leads a new life must be different from the man of the world. He must not only receive but live his new divine life. He must live up to the glory of that new life, received in Baptism and renewed to greater newness by his heavenly deeds. "The inward man is renewed day by day." [55] We are new beings every day. The renewal of our divine life is continuous and progressive as that life grows daily through our holy acts. How comforting is this fact—that, as we age daily toward the grave, there is a renewal of eternal youth, a steady growth of never-dying life within us! Ours is a new life, growing into ever newer life here and the eternal newness of Heaven.

[54] Rom. 6:4.
[55] II Cor. 4:16.

CHAPTER TEN: *An Interior Life*

I

THE new life which sanctifying grace gives to our souls is also an interior life. This means that it is a life lived principally within us. For the living grace of holiness, which is our divine life, actually dwells within our soul. Moreover, it penetrates our whole soul, so that we are not merely considered holy by God or man but really possess inward holiness. So great is the interior change wrought in the soul as it passes from the old life of sin to the new life of grace!

The Jews hoped that the kingdom of the Messias would be one of outward power and pomp and glory. However, Jesus founded a kingdom in which the members are bound to Himself by the inward ties of grace and faith and love. Thus our divine life is internal. Our Lord teaches us this when at the Last Supper He calls Himself the Vine and us the branches. On that occasion Jesus tells us: "Abide in me and I in you." [56] Now, what

[56] John 15:4.

is our abiding in Christ and His abiding in us? It is our partaking of that grace which our Savior has in its fulness; it is the like grace in Christ and in ourselves; it is the divine life within our souls—and Jesus commands us to have that life "in you," that is, interiorly. Our divine life, flowing into our souls from Christ, is an inward life, like the living sap of the vine within the branches.

We can see, therefore, how every holy person takes on himself the interior life of our Savior. "For as many of you as have been baptized in Christ have put on Christ." [57] Even the infant just baptized shares in the sanctifying grace which Our Lord has within Him, while the adult takes on more fully the interior life of Christ. In fact, adults live the divine life only when they possess this larger share of Christ's inward life; in other words, when besides sharing His grace they also have thoughts like His, pray as He prayed, love and desire what He loved and desired, feel as He did, have virtue like His.

In this manner, our soul, taking on the interior Christ, lives its own interior life of sanctity. To bring this about, the grace of holiness floods with divine life not only our soul but also its inward powers, our mind and will. Thereupon these powers help us to do many supernatural deeds that are themselves interior. For instance, our mind thinks holy thoughts, believes in the truths of the Creed, prays, plans a better life, meditates on sacred subjects, is recollected in God's presence. Our will loves with a sacred love, hopes for God's gifts, resolves to do better, sorrows for sin, aspires to Heaven, desires holy

[57] Gal. 3:27.

55

things, welcomes the Eucharistic Savior, and so on. All these inward deeds of faith and charity are fruits of the interior life within the soul. They make us, as St. Paul says, "the inward man" [58] who has faith in his heart and is rooted in charity.

Ours is an interior life of intimacy with the Blessed Trinity dwelling in our soul. In fact, our grace-life mirrors the spiritual and interior life of the triune God. Within the Trinity the Father, the Son and the Holy Spirit know and love each other in eternal union. By faith, hope and charity the man of God knows, trusts and loves the triune God and so imitates the interior life of the Holy Trinity.

Hence we rightly call our divine life an interior life. Indeed, is it not within us that the real man of God always is? The true soldier is not found in the uniform he wears, in the medals on his breast, in the signs of his rank, but in the heart of courage, in the resourceful mind, in the patriotic will filled with love for the homeland. So too the supernatural man is not marked only by the medal around his neck, the Holy Name badge on his coat, the religious garb, the priestly collar; but by what is within—first, by the soul alive with grace, and then by devotion of heart to Mary, by reverence of mind for the Holy Name, by consecration through the vows, by the sacramental character of Orders in a priest's soul. To put it briefly, the supernatural man is marked by the interior divine life within his soul. In fact, so true is this that even without the medal, without the badge, without the habit,

[58] Eph. 3:16–17.

without the collar, we can still live the divine life of holiness—because that life is, first of all, an interior life.

For our Christ-life is within us: "Christ liveth in me." [59] It is within the sanctified soul that God and man meet in mutual love. That meeting is private, hidden from the world. No matter how heavy the flow of world-traffic about a holy person, his soul is a heaven where God and he live together, converse and love each other. That is our interior life in action. That is what makes one an interior man, even in the world's busiest and loudest spot. That is our hidden life: "Your life is hid with Christ in God." [60] That is the secret, sacred love-life of God and man within the holy soul. That is the interior union of the soul with God. "To walk with God within and to be bound by no affection from without, is the state of the man of interior life." [61]

II

Although our life of grace is mainly interior, it is also exterior. Of course, the living center of our life, sanctifying grace itself, remains internal and hidden but it does bear fruit in external works of holiness. Indeed, it is only human for man, made of body as well as of soul, to show in the flesh what he feels inwardly. This is true of holy persons especially, for in them the interior life of grace is pictured in an exterior life of virtue.

How then is our divine life an exterior life? It is exterior inasmuch as our visible deeds of sanctity spring

[59] Gal. 2:20.
[60] Col. 3:3.
[61] Thomas à Kempis, *Imitation of Christ*, Book II, Chap. 6.

from the interior life of grace in our souls. Our divine life is external because it bears fruit in virtuous acts that can be noticed by all men. The life of faith, love and devotion within us shows itself in our external works of faith, love and devotion: for example, in our visible profession of faith, in our charity to our fellow men, in our public offering of Sunday Mass, in our receiving of the sacraments, in all our outward works of virtue. We need not say here how helpful it is to Catholic unity and good example that our interior life shows itself exteriorly; what we now stress is the fact itself, that our life of sanctifying grace is also an exterior life.

In truth, our grace-life must be exterior. The Catholic Church in her rites and members and works must be external so that she can be noticed by men and accepted as the one true Church. The individual Catholic, moreover, has the duty of portraying by outward deeds his inward life of holiness. "So let your light shine before men that they may see your good works and glorify your Father who is in heaven." [62] Jesus made His outward deeds of virtue prove to the bystanders His love for men, His union with the Father, His obedience to Him, and His love for Him. We other Christs must let the light of grace and faith and charity burst into visible flames that will help dispel the darkness of sin and unbelief and hatred and that will guide other souls to the Catholic Church. Such is the power of holy example by which we carry out our duty of edifying others, influence them for good, let them see our virtuous deeds and draw them to imitate our actions and so to honor God. Some Cath-

[62] Matt. 5:16.

olics fear to profess their faith openly before men; God's actual grace and His gift of fortitude will bring such men the courage to do external deeds of devotion boldly and thereby practice their religion outwardly. "For with the heart we believe unto justice; but with the mouth confession is made unto salvation." [63]

Yet our divine life is not merely exterior. It is not merely a life of the body but it is a spiritual life too. It is a life to be lived not merely in the eyes of the world but also in the sight of God. The man, therefore, whose actions merely look holy, is not living the true life of grace. Yet how many persons with hidden sins have spent their energy in preserving the outward appearance of holiness! That is why our Savior condemned those who prayed and fasted only "that they may be seen by men." [64] "This people honoreth me with their lips: but their heart is far from me." [65] Herein lies the danger of activity that is virtuous only on the outside: it can mean, as it did for the scribes and Pharisees, that "within you are full of rapine and uncleanness." [66] No wonder the Son of God called these men "hypocrites" and "whited sepulchres," [67] whose entire concern was merely to appear holy. Indeed, such external virtue is a false religion. For, while the divine life within the soul must blossom with external deeds of sanctity, these outward actions are not the whole life of holiness.

Moreover, exterior works form not even the principal

[63] Rom. 10:10.
[64] Matt. 6:5, 16.
[65] Matt. 15:8.
[66] Matt. 23:25.
[67] Matt. 23:27.

part of our grace-life. In living this life we are not concerned mainly with taking on the exterior life of Our Lord, apart from His interior life. In truth, those men are deceived who in their Christ-life stress the outward apostolate more than the inward life of holiness. For our divine life is not principally a life of "our outward man" [68]—a life of the flesh, the senses, the body. In His Sermon on the Mount our Savior commanded [69] us not to be solicitous about food or drink or clothing but to "seek . . . first the kingdom of God and his justice." [70] Our first concern, therefore, must be, not any external activity, but that share of God's justice by which we live the inward life of justifying grace.

What, then, do we conclude about our divine life? It must be interior and at the same time must show itself in exterior deeds of virtue. It is not an exterior life only, nor is it even mainly exterior. Neither is it only interior, though it is principally interior. Hence it is a life both interior and exterior but with a living bond between the two; that is, the interior life must bear fruit in the outward act of virtue while the outward act must be rooted in the inward life of grace. Together the exterior and the interior make up our divine life in action; of the two, however, the latter is far more important. For it is the interior life alone which gives divine value to our exterior actions. On the one hand, it is only when the exterior is joined to the interior that our wearing of medal or badge or religious habit has any meaning for God and

[68] II Cor. 4:16.
[69] Matt. 6:25 ff.
[70] Matt. 6:23.

men. On the other hand, all the external activity of mankind, without the life of grace, is useless for eternity. It cannot save a single soul. Hence, what God wants in us is our interior supernatural life—not any merely outward raiment or adornment or position or honor, but the inward life of sanctity visible to men through the outward acts of virtue it fosters.

CHAPTER ELEVEN: *A Life of Growth*

I

St. PAUL tells us that the sacred mystery of our baptism includes a death and a birth. We die to our old self of sin and we are born to a completely new life. We are baptized "in the likeness of" [71] Christ's death and resurrection. "Know you not that all we who are baptized in Christ Jesus, are baptized in his death? For we are buried together with him by baptism into death: that as Christ is risen from the dead . . . so we also may walk in newness of life." [72] Jesus died in His mortal life; in death He was buried; then He rose from the dead to His new and immortal life. This death and resurrection of our Savior every Baptism vividly represents, though it is easier to see this sacred representation in the Baptism of the early Church. During those ages the candidate for divine life was submerged in the baptismal water and then he emerged from the water to a new life of grace.

[71] Rom. 6:5.
[72] Rom. 6:3–4.

What meets the eye in such a ceremony is the submerging and the emerging of a person. But this is a Christian sacrament, a sacred rite with sacred meaning and power. What then is meant by the submerging of the candidate? First, it represents in holy likeness the death and burial of our Savior. Moreover, it pictures the death to sin and the burial of self which the one being baptized undergoes in holy imitation of Our Lord. "For we are buried together with him by baptism into death." Lastly, Baptism not only pictures but actually brings about this very death and burial of self. In Baptism we die "with Christ"; [73] we die to our sinful selves. And it is the sacrament that causes this death, for it takes away from our soul every sin—mortal and venial, one and all. Thus Baptism in the likeness of Christ's death makes us "dead to sin." [74]

But there is another part to the sacrament, namely, the emerging from the water. What does this mean for the person being baptized? First, it represents in holy likeness Our Lord's resurrection from the dead to His new life. Secondly, it pictures the rising to the divine life of sanctity which the newly baptized start to live in holy imitation of our Savior: "As Christ is risen from the dead . . . so we also may walk in newness of life." Lastly, this new and divine life Baptism not only pictures but actually begets within us. For the sacrament gives us our first grace of holiness; we are born of the baptismal water into the new and divine life. Thus Baptism "in the

[73] Rom. 6:8.
[74] Rom. 6:2.

63

likeness of his resurrection" [75] makes us "alive unto God in Christ Jesus Our Lord." [76]

In this way Baptism is a death and a resurrection. This is true of every Christian baptism even when received by the unconscious, by the dying or by the unknowing infant. Hence the Baptism of today does two things: it causes our death to sin and it enlivens our soul with the divine life of grace.

From our birth into the divine life we properly advance to the next step, our growth in that life. It is God's design that growth should follow birth in every kind of life. Furthermore, God wishes us to grow especially in the life of grace: "And he that is just, let him be justified still: and he that is holy, let him be sanctified still." [77]

Yet how shall we grow in the divine life? We were born into this life through a death and a resurrection, through a submerging of self and a rising above self, through a dying of our sinful self and a rising of our new self. We shall grow in our divine life through a continued dying to our sinful self and a continued rising above self.

Hence, if we would have our divine life grow, we must constantly die to self at least as far as mortal sin is concerned. We must continually repress the inward self that invites us to such sin; we must continually crush our pride. In contrition we must often strike our breast and in adoration we must often bow our knee to the earth. We must subject our body to penance, we must humble

[75] Rom. 6:5.
[76] Rom. 6:11.
[77] Apoc. 22:11.

our mind in faith, we must bend our will in obedience to God. We must, as far as need be, take self out of all our deeds and we must reject every enticement of serious temptation. Finally, in all matters of moment for our soul, we must ever renounce Satan, his works and his pomps.

This continued submerging of our nature means a daily dying to our selves. Daily, as we did at Baptism, we cease to live in our selfish selves—and ceasing to live is dying! Daily, as we did at Baptism, we give up our old life of sin—and giving up life is dying! This, then, is the way in which we shall die in order that our divine life may grow.

In addition, we must continue to rise above our former self. At the least, we must fulfill our serious obligations to God and to men; and in doing so, we shall always rise superior to our weak, human, tempted self. For we must pray to God; we must devoutly follow Our Lord; we must imitate Our Lady and the saints; we must love our neighbor in word and work. "Seek ye therefore first the kingdom of God," [78] Jesus commands us. We must labor to live the higher life. We must continually hope for and strive to obtain Heaven; we must often use those heavenly helps, prayer and the sacraments; and we must daily do deeds of supernatural holiness, that is, works above mere human strength and virtue.

In this way we constantly rise above our natural self. We continue to do what we did at Baptism—rise with Christ to a higher life. "Therefore, if you be risen with

[78] Matt. 6:33.

Christ, seek the things that are above." [79] We perform works entirely beyond mere human power: we labor for Heaven, we imitate Jesus and Mary, we receive Holy Communion, we offer Christ in sacrifice to the Father, we love all men, we use God's actual grace and we fulfill our serious obligations. This is a way of life beyond mere flesh and blood; and by this way we continually rise above our human selves.

The manner of acting just described is surely a continued death and resurrection. Now, as we already noted, it is precisely through this constant dying to self and rising above self that the divine life of grace thrives within a man's soul. Hence we too by a program of spiritual death and resurrection with Christ will certainly enlarge our supernatural life begun at Baptism. "But grow in grace," [80] God tells us; and it is ours to do that all our days.

Here, while we consider our growth as sons of God, it will help us to read a verse from St. John: "Whosoever is born of God, committeth not sin, for his seed abideth in him." [81] The seed of God which the Apostle mentions is sanctifying grace. This grace St. John calls God's seed because it is the germ of divine life within us. As sons "born of God," we rightly possess His seed. Let us see how truly the grace of holiness is a seed.

For all living creatures on this earth a seed is first life. A seed is the beginning of individual life and the point whence all growth toward maturity starts. A seed is the

[79] Col. 3:1.
[80] II Peter 3:18.
[81] I John 3:9.

first step in the process of life. Now, for those "born of God" through Baptism, the sanctifying grace then received is truly a seed. For that grace is the first unit of divine life generated in us by God. It is the first cell of our new life. When among men a child is conceived, a seed of human life is planted within the earth of human flesh. So too when we are begotten of the heavenly Father, sanctifying grace as the seed of heavenly life is planted within us. That first grace is the beginning of our supernatural life and the starting point of all spiritual growth.

Secondly, a seed is a tiny beginning. The seeds we know best are those of certain fruits, grains, and flowers. Such seed is generally small, for example, the grain of wheat. We can hold it in our fingers. It is dull in appearance; it looks unimportant; it shows no sign of life at all. Yet it teems with life and with the promise of more life. That seed can grow into still fuller life, into the mature plant and the ripe harvest. Truly a rich life throbs in the dull, helpless seed!

So likewise sanctifying grace in the newly baptized is a tiny beginning. Let us, for example, suppose that a foreign missionary has just baptized an infant, a leper and a dying native, and that at the same moment a priest in our land has baptized a college professor, a banker and a newspaper editor. These persons, fresh from the waters of Baptism, differ in many ways—in age, language, riches, learning and culture. They seem, after receiving the sacrament, to be entirely the same as before; for instance, they retain their personal differences. Their life appears unchanged. Outwardly they give no hint at all of enjoying a higher life. Yet they have all been changed remarkably. They have received God's seed, a first tiny share of sanctifying grace. From the moment of their spiritual generation through Baptism they have been divinely alive. Children of men, they are now infant children of God. Into their bodies, sick or healthy, has come a more abundant life, rich with the promise of virtue and glory. The seed of divine life within their breasts has a beauty and brilliance and vitality beyond man's power to dream of or to invent. That brilliance no man could bear to see unaided, so rich is the tiny beginning of heavenly life in our baptismal grace!

Lastly, the life within a seed is very incomplete, like the first cell of infant life in a mother's body. If a seed remain a seed, it has little value. If we keep a grain of wheat in an envelope, "itself remaineth alone"; [82] there is no continued life, no increase, no harvest. How then does a seed have value? The answer is that seeds, as God made them, can and should grow into full life, into tall corn, the fruit tree, the giant redwood and the mature man. The young life of the acorn should steadily progress into the perfect life of the oak tree. The life in the young seed and in the old plant always remains identical; but the seed must, through constant growth, increase unto the complete life of maturity.

In like manner, sanctifying grace in those just baptized is also incomplete. To tell the truth, our divine life is incomplete all our days on earth. For not merely after Baptism but at any time up to death can the grace of

[82] John 12:25.

holiness increase within us. In fact, God wants it to increase. The infant child of God, freshly born into the divine life, must grow into the man of God alive with an abundance of grace. Thus our baptismal grace should steadily progress into ever greater saintliness, into virtue, into spiritual wisdom and vigor, into holy works that earn Heaven for us, into the power to conquer temptation, into eternal glory, "unto a perfect man, unto the measure of the age of the fulness of Christ." [83] While our sanctifying grace remains identical through all this advance, our divine life has passed from infancy to fulness. God's seed has grown into its complete supernatural life. "The just shall flourish like the palm tree: he shall grow up like the cedar of Libanus. They that are planted in the house of the Lord shall flourish in the courts of the house of our God. They shall still increase in a fruitful old age." [84]

II

The day we are baptized is the birthday of our divine life. From that date we count our years as sons of God. Baptism may have come to us as babes of a few days, in middle life, in old age or finally on our deathbed; yet it gave us for the first time sanctifying grace, and this first gift of divine life made us spiritual infants. Even old men, newly baptized, are in God's sight only spiritual babes. So St. Peter calls those born of God through Baptism "newborn babes." [85]

[83] Eph. 4:13.
[84] Psalm 91:13–15.
[85] I Peter 2:2.

In the human family infants are made to live their life and to grow in that life. God by no means wants us to remain infants all our days. Rather, He wishes us to use our eyes, our mind, our hands and our other powers, to grow by using them and to make of ourselves the best men possible. God wants us to grow in our human life from infancy to full manhood. It was thus in His humanity that Jesus advanced in wisdom and age with God and men.

But we are talking about man's spiritual infancy. At the first moment that the waters of Baptism bring us sanctifying grace, we become "newborn babes," children of God with a divine life. Here too God does not want us to remain spiritual infants all our days. He has given a common vocation to each of us; and that vocation is for us to be born of Himself into a divine life, to live that life, to grow in it and to perfect ourselves in it. The infant son of God must begin to use the supernatural powers which the Father gave him at birth, must perform deeds of Christlike virtue and so must increase his divine vitality unto spiritual manhood. "Crave, as newborn babes, pure spiritual milk, that by it you may grow to salvation." [86]

This command the saints of God through the centuries have obeyed and thus they increased their divine life. Among us, the infant grows through childhood and adolescence into full manhood and a ripe old age; in like manner, the supernatural infant must grow through a spiritual childhood and adolescence into the full virtue of supernatural manhood. So Mary advanced from the

[86] I Peter 2:2 (Confraternity of Christian Doctrine version).

first moment of grace-life at her Immaculate Conception through her young years, when she was hailed "full of grace," [87] to her Assumption into glory. So the Apostles grew from spiritual childhood in Our Lord's first training-school to a mature life of virtue, crowned with martyrdom. Thus too did St. Paul increase his Christ-life from the day of his conversion to his death, so that he could say: "I live, now not I: but Christ liveth in me." [88] For Mary and the Apostles this growth in the divine life was no sudden jump but a constant increase won at the expense of constant virtuous deeds.

The true Church has begotten thousands of saints who have followed different paths of holiness. Among these saints we number widows, virgins, confessors, martyrs and popes. We have saints of the home, the school, the throne, the convent, the priesthood and the seminary; of youth, the religious orders and the foreign missions; of labor, matrimony and suffering. Moreover, there are saints of every virtue—of courage, faith, love and sorrow for sin; of purity, silence, mortification and charity toward one's neighbor; of poverty, reparation, prayer and Eucharistic adoration. Clearly the Holy Spirit has led the saints along diverse roads of godliness. For each saint He has designed a personal path of virtue; then through His actual grace He has shown each saint this chosen path, has guided him along it and has given him the strength to follow the path of holiness to its end. Some saints, like Agnes and Stanislaus, accomplished much in a short space, and these as youths had grown in the divine

[87] Luke 1:28.
[88] Gal. 2:20.

life even to heroic sanctity. Other saints are said to have preserved their baptismal innocence, and in these the grace-life had a steady growth from spiritual infancy to spiritual manhood. Finally, other saints have lived in sin for a long time, like Augustine and Magdalen; but once they received sanctifying grace, they became giants of saintliness and their divine life bore fruit in heroic contrition and love. Now, varied as are the saints of God, the purpose of all their good works, words and example was always that they might grow in the divine life, in the same grace which Christ had and which all, as other Christs, have. The saints ever made it their business, their lifework and their joy to grow steadily in the life of grace.

We too must grow in our divine life. We must daily live this life. An infant in the human family needs to be waited on; he requires all manner of help; he receives everything. But wise parents teach him early to use his hands and feet and tongue so that he will learn to help himself and to live his own life. The supernatural infant too, fresh from Baptism, has received all kinds of help. He possesses the divine life of grace; he houses within himself the Blessed Trinity; he is armed with the supernatural strength of faith, hope and charity. When he has the use of reason, he begins to employ these virtues in prayer, in offering the Holy Sacrifice, in love of neighbor; and thus he starts to live and to enlarge his grace-life. For life is action. When action stops, it is a sign that death has set in. To be alive means we must show the life within us by our activity. Hence we must be continually active if we would continue living our divine life.

Moreover, the human person must live up to his life as a man. Since life is action, he must act in a way befitting his dignity as a reasonable creature—a dignity because of which God placed man above all other earthly beings. Indeed, when a person behaves against sound reason, we say he has degraded himself; he does not deserve to be called a man; he acts like an animal; he is not living up to his life as a man. The supernatural man too must live up to his divine life. He must act in a way worthy of his life as God's son. Indeed, not to do this when he faces serious temptation is a mortal sin and a deadly illness in his divine life; it means the supernatural man is not living up to his nobilty as a member of God's family. Hence the child of God must, under threat of hell-fire, perform the virtuous deeds required to avoid mortal sin. But this is the least that our life of grace demands of us. In all past ages holy souls have appreciated man's vocation to saintliness and so they lived the divine life to its fullest. In like manner, we too must, by our supernatural acts of virtue, live up to the divine life within us.

Thus to live our divine life we must constantly do deeds which have a divine value. We must act in obedience to God; we must do what pleases God; we must perform deeds which God will accept as worthy of a divine reward. In truth, it is precisely by such deeds that the saints on earth both maintain and enlarge their life of grace. Those who are alive with the supernatural vitality of sanctifying grace merit by their holy works to grow in that supernatural vitality. By each act of virtue they live their divine life a little more fully; they gain in strength to do holier deeds; their sanctity is greater; they deserve a richer reward in Heaven. Through our virtuous activity we build up our grace-life, we possess more divine life. This is the increase of our supernatural life which God in His goodness deigns to give us because of deeds well done.

For the Father who begot us as His children wills that we must work with Him in order to reach the prime of our supernatural life. Then, for each good deed—even for works of obligation—He grants His child to grow in the divine life. This God does because, in His sight, the virtuous deeds which holy souls freely choose to do with His help merit an increase in the grace of life. The rate of that increase in the divine life is measured by our sanctity as children of God, the greatness of the holy deeds we do and the warmth of virtue with which we do them. "He who soweth sparingly, shall also reap sparingly: and he who soweth in blessings, shall also reap blessings." [89] Of course the sacraments, the Holy Sacrifice and prayer advance our divine life most. In particular, the Holy Eucharist, as being truly the divine food and drink of our souls, nourishes us with a more abundant life.

An example of growth in the divine life comes to us from three centuries ago. Father Druillettes, a French Jesuit, worked among the Catholic Algonquin Indians. After spending the winter of 1647-1648 with his flock, the missionary said of the Indians: "The savages with

[89] II Cor. 9:6.

74

whom I wintered are no longer children in the faith. I have found constancy in them and entire trust in all dangers. They have a deeper devotion toward the holy Sacrifice of the Mass than before; they have proved themselves more courteous and gentle toward me than ever before and surely God has been a most loving and special Father to them all." [90]

Clearly the child of God, simply by acting as a Catholic, can grow to spiritual manhood in his Christ-life; and while he grows, his outward actions will picture the increased vitality of his interior life. The man of God will exhibit the manly virtues of self-control, temperance, strong faith, zeal for souls, courage and active charity. He will spurn temptation more readily. He will think more often of God and God's cause; he will be more recollected in his prayer; he will receive the sacraments more frequently, fervently and fruitfully. The person in the prime of his supernatural life does more holy deeds—more in number, fervor, devotion, virtue and love. In this manner he perseveres in sanctifying grace and lives his divine life more deeply and richly.

So through all his years the man of God can live an ever-enlarging life of grace as his holiness approaches the holiness of Christ. What a wonderful sight it is before God that, as our bodily life declines, our divine life grows! As our human life begins to die, our heavenly life is more vigorous and sublime. While our eyes dim, our faith stays strong. Our hearing departs, but we are alive to the call of God's actual grace. Our steps falter, yet we walk more surely the way of divine life. While

[90] *The Jesuit Relations*, edited by Thwaites, XXXII, 275.

our body fails, the vitality of our supernatural virtue increases. Slowly the bond between body and soul weakens. Though the frail body can scarcely support the soul, the divine life within that soul is strong.

These last moments are most important. It matters little that our death be peaceful, violent, lonely, ignoble, sudden or with friends—as long as that death be holy. Death must crown our life, not merely end it. Then the last moment, when we have lived long in God's grace, will find our soul at its peak of supernatural vigor, the climax of its steady growth in the divine life. "Be thou faithful until death: and I will give thee the crown of life." [91]

[91] Apoc. 2:10.

CHAPTER TWELVE : *An Eternal Life*

Man's soul is immortal. God made it to live forever —somewhere. United with our flesh, it dwells on earth till we die; then, in the case of persons attaining the use of reason, the soul lives eternally either in Heaven or in Hell.

Thus our soul can look to an eternal life as its own right. But we do not speak here of the soul leading its natural life after its earthly existence. We are not speaking of continued life as the natural right of the soul. Even in a place of endless torment the human soul lives its immortal life. What we are considering is eternal life as the true, higher, eternal life, the eternal life of Heaven. This is indeed life eternal, for Hell is really eternal death.

We speak, therefore, of the heavenly eternity which is our supernatural destiny. But how is our divine life of grace an eternal life? Because it is actually our heavenly

77

reward, our blessed happiness? No. What, then, do we mean by saying our divine life here is an eternal life?

The life of grace within the soul is an eternal life inasmuch as it is a beginning of our eternal life in Heaven. When we possess sanctifying grace in our soul, we have started our life of blessedness. Our life in Heaven is the fulness and the crowning of our sanctifying grace here; the grace of holiness is the beginning of our life eternal.

That beginning of eternal life is first had through Baptism, wherein we are begotten of the Father unto the divine life of grace. So great is God's goodness that in His designs for us we can begin our eternal life here. Of course the life of grace will be perfected in Heaven. The dimness of divine faith will yield to the clear vision of God; our charity will be climaxed by the satisfying love of God; our supernatural joy here will give way to the complete happiness of Heaven.

Yet the life of the blessed in Heaven is not a higher kind of life than our grace-life here. Animal life stands a world above the life of a flower; but no such difference separates our soul's divine life on earth from our life in Heaven. Both these lives—if we may speak of them as separate lives—are beyond any other created life; both are of a supernatural order; both are, of all lives, the nearest to God's own life; both are on the identical level of life. In fact, they are one and the same life—begun in grace here and reaching its height in glory forever. Thus the infant baptized, the sinner forgiven, everyone in the state of grace—all these have actually started to live their eternal life. Indeed, they need only die in order to reach their everlasting glory, so truly is our divine life here a beginning of our eternal life!

This our Savior tells us, using the words "eternal life," "everlasting life." By these terms He sometimes meant our heavenly reward. "It is better for thee to enter lame into life everlasting than having two feet to be cast into the hell of unquenchable fire." [92] "And these shall go into everlasting punishment: but the just into life everlasting." [93] At other times Our Lord called the divine life of grace on earth an eternal life. "He who heareth my word and believeth him that sent me, hath life everlasting." [94] The holy soul, believing in God, already has an eternal life. "He that eateth my flesh and drinketh my blood hath everlasting life." [95] The person worthily receiving the Eucharist already lives a life everlasting. "Now this is eternal life: that they may know thee, the only true God." [96] The man of faith possesses eternal life. But belief in God and the reception of Holy Communion take place only on this earth; they do not occur in Heaven. So Jesus teaches us that souls, sanctified in virtue and by the receiving of the sacraments, have already started to live their life everlasting. Our divine life even on earth is our eternal life already begun.

Moreover, in yet another way our grace-life may be an eternal life. For God set no limit on the length of our divine life; rather, He wished it to go on as everlastingly as the soul which it enlivens. Here Christ, the Life, offers

[92] Mark 9:44.
[93] Matt. 25:46.
[94] John 5:24.
[95] John 6:55.
[96] John 17:3.

Himself as our model. He died once [97] to die no more, but to live eternally. So too we in Baptism die once to sin, are born to new life and are called to live that new life ever after.

Thus our divine life can and should be eternal. Once we begin this life at the baptismal font, we should continue in it all our earthly days and live it forever in Heaven. This is God's will for us; and only man himself interferes with that will when, through mortal sin, he loses the grace of life. Such a one started to live the life eternal and then faltered badly. Of course he can, by means of the sacraments, regain the grace of holiness; he can even increase that grace within himself; he can begin again to live the full grace-life here and hereafter. For by God's goodness our divine life can be our eternal life not merely begun but continued here till death and afterward in Heaven.

Actually, some of God's heroes have carried their divine life through from Baptism to death. We say they preserved their baptismal innocence. They began life eternal at their soul-birth and unfailingly carried it into Heaven. Thus they made their days here a paradise, a heaven on earth. Their earthly span was a paradise because they preserved the great gift which made this world a paradise for Adam—the grace of divine life and holiness. Their life here was also a heaven because all their years they dwelt in eternal life. No matter what sorrows they suffered here, they made their earthly span what God wants it to be—a heaven on earth.

This high holiness God sets as a goal for all men. How

[97] Rom. 6:8–11.

heavenly, then, is the soul that receives the grace of life at Baptism and never loses it! Such a person goes through his entire mortal existence without sinning grievously; indeed, he constantly enlarges his divine life. It will be to his glory in Heaven that he never lost the grace of life.

Of course many persons do lose the grace of holiness through mortal sin. For them God's wish is that in the confessional they again receive sanctifying grace and that thus they again start on their eternal life and persevere in it forever. Numerous are the sainted penitents now in Heaven who started and restarted their eternal life here till, finally using the graces of perseverance, they merited to continue their life eternal in Heaven. For such also as these the world at last became a Heaven on earth and their grace-life an eternal life.

In two ways, then, may we rightly view our life of holiness as an eternal life. It is a start on our life everlasting; that life everlasting in Heaven is its fulness and crowning. Secondly, our grace-life can and should endure eternally. Any serious failure in that life turns our soul toward eternal death; perseverance in it means an eternal life of blessedness with God. We can here use the words of the beloved Disciple: "These things I write to you that you may know that you have eternal life, you who believe in the name of the Son of God." [98]

[98] I John 5:13.

CHAPTER THIRTEEN: *A Sacramental Life*

I

OUR Savior came to earth so that men might live the more abundant life of grace. Giving us this divine vocation, He gave us all the help needed to carry it out. Our main help is found in the seven sacraments, which have been well adapted by Our Lord for our receiving them and for our growth in holiness through them. In general they are made up of words and actions which deal with familiar objects such as water, oil, wine and bread; and at the same time they, along with God, produce a spiritual, supernatural fruit within our soul, that is, the grace of divine life.

Indeed, the sacraments of the New Testament were planned by Christ on the basis of life; their real value lies in the life which they give us. Now, through all the levels of life, from the smallest flower to Almighty God, one life parallels another—though at the same time with varying differences. This is true of our life which is the fruit of the sacraments, that is, our grace-life. Thus our divine life is built on our human life, uses it, parallels it and perfects it. Let us see the parallel.

Our earthly life is one of birth and growth. For years, nourishment builds our bodies and study increases the powers of our souls. We repair the daily wear on our bodies' cells, we heal our bruises and cuts, we overcome disease and we fight off even death. In the interval we have grown to manhood and played our part in passing on human life to our children. Gradually the strength to repair our bodies ceases, we lapse into old age and the body, no longer fit to house the soul, dies.

Our divine life begins in like manner with a birth: our birth as children of God. Thence follows a life of growth which, as in our earthly life, may be constant or may be retarded. While our constant advance in holiness will reach its fullest growth at the moment of bodily death, as God ordained for all men, we can go on living that life in Heaven for all eternity. Our grace-life can be retarded either by spiritual weakness, such as venial sin, evil habits and a lack of generosity, or by the deadly malady of mortal sin. In these lapses of our divine life we can, by God's goodness, repair our spiritual weakness and sickness; yes, even on the brink of ever-lasting death in Hell, we can always ward off eternal damnation and live the life of grace here and hereafter.

Of course, too, there are differences between our merely human life and our divine life; they are not perfectly alike. For instance, the human infant has lived only a short time, whereas the spiritual infant, just born of God in Baptism, may be a person on in years. We have heard of such a one baptized late in life, numbering his years from the day when through Baptism he became a son of God. Again, the child of this world needs years of experience to be a mature man, yet God's children can advance to mature sanctity at an early age. Witness God's child-saints. Blessed Imelda, on fire with love of the Eucharist, entered the Dominican Sisters when ten years old. Receiving her first Holy Communion miraculously at the age of eleven, she died immediately afterward—out of love of her Eucharistic God. Saint Stanislaus Kostka attained sainthood in less than eighteen years. In 1902 Saint Maria Goretti, only eleven years old, died in defense of her purity like another St. Agnes. St. Thomas Kosaki was a fourteen-year-old Japanese lad who died in 1597. Though he could have escaped if he had wanted, he preferred to be put into prison and to die by crucifixion with the priest whose altar-boy and companion he had been. Blessed Dominic Savio died in 1857 when not yet fifteen years of age. He became holy by living the everyday life of an Italian schoolboy. A confessor of the faith, a model of purity and a disciple of St. John Bosco, he was beatified in 1950.

We now notice a third difference between our merely human life and our grace-life. Our flesh-and-blood life may thrive without holiness; on the other hand, our divine life flourishes on holiness alone. Furthermore, our bodily life must suffer and die. Our supernatural life need never suffer the spiritual paralysis of mortal sin or the spiritual death of Hell. Some of God's holy ones have carried their baptismal innocence to Heaven. Lastly, as our human life weakens and dies, our grace-life glories in its full power to do virtuous deeds and to win Heaven. But despite such differences, our human life and our divine life show a parallel in many steps of their life-processes. For in both lives we find these features of true life: birth, growth, repair, nourishment, strength, maturity, family, reproduction and fatherhood.

We said our Savior intended that the sacraments should confer life—indeed, a higher life which would dwell with and work with our human life. Accordingly, our sacraments do give us life, a divine life paralleling our natural life. This is not our bodily life, which can grow to fulness and old age without sacraments at all; but it is our grace-life, our heavenly life, the divine life of our soul. Thus the sacraments are the common means we use for growing in holiness. Of their own power under God, they—for example, water and the words of Baptism; oil and the words of Confirmation—produce the higher life within us; they give us sanctifying grace, they recover it when lost and they increase it up to our last moment on earth; and by nourishing us spiritually, they strengthen and enlarge our supernatural life. "The sacraments," Pope Pius XII writes, "are rivers of divine grace and of divine life." [99]

Baptism, for example, starts us on our new life. For in it we are born again of water and the Holy Spirit so that our souls become holy spirits. Moreover, because through Baptism we are begotten of God, we begin to live a divine life. Our soul is filled with its first share of sanctifying grace, its first spark of supernatural life. The newly baptized person, however short or long his

[99] Encyclical *Mediator Dei.*

earthly existence, is an infant member of God's family. So Baptism begets us as God's own children, graced with the newborn life of holiness.

In addition, Baptism of water—and it alone—gives us a right to receive the other sacraments. Thus our higher life, begun by Baptism, is strengthened and increased by the six remaining sacraments. In converts to the Church the grace-life grows immediately after their Baptism, because, having the use of reason, they can at once do holy deeds and receive other sacraments. Little children, however, while they truly possess the divine life, begin to live it actively and to grow in it only at the age of reason. Let us now observe the life-giving work of the sacraments received after Baptism.

II

In observing the work of the sacraments received after Baptism, we must note that during this chapter we shall speak only of persons who enjoy the use of reason, who through Baptism have a right to the other sacraments, who already live the life of grace and who therefore can grow in their Christ-life.

To such souls Confirmation, a sacrament of growth and strength, brings further divine life and vigor. In a human family the infant first receives everything; then as he grows, he is trained to help himself and his family. In Baptism the infant child of God has likewise received everything from his Father, even to a share in God's life and love; now through Confirmation he gains strength in his grace-life and he faces his future years, prepared to live an active life of holiness for himself and his Church. In Confirmation God's infant son becomes a young man of God, strengthened for a steady advance in virtue.

In our journey through this world our body requires daily nourishment; in addition, at times of stress and sickness, our food and drink must be carefully chosen to ensure us the special vitality we need. For our divine life, the Holy Eucharist offers us a lifelong nourishment; furthermore, in the face of temptations and evil habits and bad example, it assures us of the divine courage and strength we so sorely need.

Our third sacrament helps us in this way because it is a sacrament of nourishment. For souls living the higher life it is supernatural food and drink. "My flesh is meat indeed and my blood is drink indeed." [100] Hence, from childhood to old age the Holy Eucharist nourishes and enlarges and delights our divine life. To Catholics whose grace-life is weak or who are children of God only a short while or who need heavenly courage or who are spiritually hungry and thirsty, this sacrament will bring growth in holiness and strength of virtue. Other Catholics, who have advanced in the grace-life and whose souls thrive on virtuous activity, the Blessed Sacrament preserves in the full vigor of divine life and leads to an ever new and richer closeness with our Savior.

For the Eucharist is God Our Lord Himself. He is our Sacrament and so it is Christ, man and God, whom we receive in Holy Communion as food and drink for our souls. No wonder that we, other Christs, draw from such godly nourishment an increased divine life and a fuller

[100] John 6:56.

87

Christ-life. In the first Paradise the fruit of the tree of life [101] would have kept Adam's body growing; our Eucharist is greater than that. It keeps the divine life growing within us, for it comes from another Tree of Life, the Cross of Calvary.

We often pray "Give us this day our daily bread." [102] We need daily food to sustain our human life; just as necessary is nourishment for our higher life. "Except you eat the flesh of the Son of man and drink his blood, you shall not have life in you." [103] Men die of hunger and thirst; without the Eucharist it seems hardly possible, under ordinary circumstances, to persevere in grace and to live actively the more abundant life. If bread can be called the staff of life, then the Blessed Sacrament is not a luxury but a necessity of our grace-life.

Of course we must receive our Eucharistic God devoutly. To draw greater strength and vitality from our ordinary food, we approach the table with health and appetite. For spiritual profit from receiving the Eucharist we must enjoy a healthy divine life free from mortal sin and we must approach the Communion table with desire and love. Then will the Blessed Sacrament strengthen us through the long pull of our earthly existence and produce in us a holy likeness to Our Lord. Truly we have in the Blessed Eucharist our greatest means of attaining maturity and sainthood in the divine life. Of this Pope Pius X assures us. "Holy Communion is the shortest and surest way to Heaven. There are others—innocence, for

[101] Gen. 2:9.
[102] Luke 11:3.
[103] John 6:54.

instance—but that is for little children; penance, but we are afraid of it; a generous endurance of the trials of life, but when they approach us, we weep and pray to be delivered. Once for all, beloved children, the surest, easiest, shortest way is by the Holy Eucharist."

Up to this point we have received the divine life through Baptism; Confirmation has strengthened it; and all our days the Eucharist will nourish it. We are well equipped to live our supernatural life. We can, in fact, preserve and grow in our individual grace of holiness as long as we live up to the rules of spiritual health.

Here again we note the parallel between our bodily life and our divine life. A person's vitality can be lowered by disease, even by the beginning of disease, and we rejoice when the doctor catches in its first stages a disease which, if not treated, would prove fatal. Again, lesser ailments slow down the course of human life. We grow weak for want of rest, fresh air and nourishment; and in those who have grown old, who suffer bodily pain, who are deaf or blind or lame—in all these life proceeds at a retarded pace.

In the spiritual order, too, the life which God's children enjoy suffers setbacks. Some of these are critical, as when by seriously violating God's laws for their supernatural well-being men fall into mortal sin. In this chapter, however, we speak not of those who through grave sin lose sanctifying grace but of those who preserve the grace of life. Such souls, while remaining holy, are sometimes guilty of venial sin and can by frequent lapses form habits of venial sin. In these circumstances, their power for good is weakened and their progress in the divine life retarded. Other obstacles also can lessen the fulness of our grace-life—for instance, an ungenerous spirit, a desire for comfort, a lack of devotion, infrequent prayer, self-seeking and a failure to use God's actual graces.

In this sickness of soul we approach the confessional. There the priest is our doctor, ministering to us through Penance, the sacrament of hope and mercy. By means of his priestly absolution this sacrament forgives our faults and imparts to us the grace that heals. Thus our sanctifying grace is increased and we become holier children of God. Our soul has been refreshed with new life and strength. The ailments which weakened its supernatural vitality have been diagnosed and treated lest, falling little by little, we lapse into the grave illness of mortal sin and the fatal illness of eternal death. In Penance, moreover, our sacramental doctor gives the prescription for maintaining spiritual health at its peak and for preserving our divine life forever. Frequently too this sacrament brings us a conscious peace of mind and joy of soul. As we leave the confessional, our heavenly life is already coursing at a quickened pace.

For the person who always chooses to reject serious temptation, the divine life grows continuously. At the same time, the passing years weaken his body; occasionally he suffers grave illness and even faces death. Now comes the most important moment for our bodily life as it lapses into death, and for our soul's grace-life as we go to meet God; and for this special occasion our Redeemer has given us the sacrament of Extreme Unction.

To the sick man this holy rite brings sanctifying grace, an injection of supernatural life for the last struggle.

Thus the grace of holiness is increased within his soul and his divine power for doing virtuous deeds is strengthened. While his bodily life falters, the life which makes him God's son grows more vigorous. The sacred anointing has given him the saving grace of life, the final sanctifying of a man about to face his Judge. In the dying person Extreme Unction has improved the soul's likeness to God so that, at judgment, this child of God will be an image of his divine Father, ready to claim his eternal reward.

Thus far we have noted how the first five sacraments influence man's personal divine life. There remain two other sacraments, Holy Orders and Matrimony, whose purpose is first the general supernatural vitality of the Church and only secondarily the individual holiness of those ordained or married.

In treating Holy Orders we shall speak of the priesthood, because that is the sacramental order best known to Catholics. This sacred ceremony of ordination gives to the living Church of God new priests—leaders, rulers, teachers and fathers of souls, who, through the sacraments, will beget and nourish the life of grace within the Catholic Church. Like St. Paul, the priest can say: "For in Christ Jesus by the gospel I have begotten you . . ." [104] "My little children, of whom I am in labor again until Christ be formed in you." [105] Rightly then do we call our priests "Father" and our Pope "Holy Father." For the Catholic priest ministers to God's children like a

[104] I Cor. 4:15.
[105] Gal. 4:19.

parent, giving and sustaining and healing and strengthening the divine life within the Mystical Body.

Called to dispense the life of holiness to his fellow men, the priest should be holy himself. Hence by Our Lord's design the ordination which confers the priestly power is also a sacrament which sanctifies the new priest. The fruit of Holy Orders is, at one and the same time, both the priesthood and holiness, so that the candidate emerges from his ordination a holy priest. Thus the sacrament increases the life of holiness within the new priest's soul and makes him a fit minister of Christ.

We have already mentioned Matrimony, the sacrament of Catholic marriage and of holy families. This sacred rite effects the marriage bond; that is, it makes man and woman husband and wife in God's household. At the same time Matrimony sanctifies those entering on their wedded vocation. Indeed, because the contracting parties are in the state of grace, this sacrament of the living increases the grace-life within the souls of the newly married couple. As they receive the right to share their human life with their children, God shares His divine life of holiness with them.

For in making the marriage ceremony a sacrament, our Savior used as a model His own union with the Catholic Church, His Mystical Body. Our Lord unites Himself to us in a supernatural union of grace and love and life and holiness; similarly husband and wife will be one, not merely through a fleshly tie, but in the supernatural bond of grace and love and life and holiness. That is why Catholic Matrimony both unites and sanctifies man and woman. Indeed, in the very rite in which Catholic spouses surrender themselves one to the other for the sacred purposes of Matrimony, one partner administers the sacrament to the other; and hence their first gift to each other is the priceless gift of sanctifying grace which the sacrament produces.

So the wedded couple start their lives together in the finest manner possible: their marriage life is a divine life of holiness. Already sanctifying grace is elevating and perfecting their human love for each other. They are spouses in Christ, alive with the Christly life in a way befitting the Catholic husband and wife. Thus they enter their marriage—holy spouses, prepared to bring forth children of God and to continue their wedded life on the divine level of virtue.

We have watched how the sacraments bestow on us the living grace of sanctity through all our earthly days. Under God they beget, nourish, repair, strengthen and increase within our souls the divine life of holiness. We can truthfully call this supernatural life a sacramental life because its birth, growth and permanence in us is the work of the seven sacraments.

III

The sacraments are the main sources of our divine life—giving it birth, strength and growth until at our death it reaches its height of holiness. Yet in maintaining that life at the divine level we need another kind of grace, the grace called "actual." Hence our Savior, who gave us the sacramental life, planned that His sacraments should also win for us certain actual graces. As a result, the Catholic today who faithfully receives a sacrament, earns for himself many actual graces which God will grant him as he needs them.

This grace helps God's children to do acts of supernatural virtue. It is a temporary assistance for the spiritual activity of the moment. It enlightens man's mind and inspires his will, showing him clearly what God wants done and at the same time urging and empowering him to do it. The grace of action aids sanctified souls to accomplish those holy deeds which carry out the high purpose of our sacramental life.

We said the person who properly receives a sacrament earns for himself certain actual graces. The fact is that the sacraments give us a right to these graces, a true claim on God Himself. Imagine having a real claim on God, a claim which He will surely honor! Of course this sacramental right comes from God's generous plan for administering the sacraments which His Son left us as the daily support of our divine life. Yet God respects that right and constantly grants us His helpful graces.

Such graces are very special indeed. They are directed, not to all points of holiness, as are actual graces in general, but to one point: the purpose of each sacrament. They are granted, not for all kinds of virtue, but for the particular virtues needed by those whom the sacraments call to special duties—the Christian, the soldier of God, the dying, the priest, the Catholic husband and wife. These sacramental graces are offered to us in order that by using them we may become holier Christians, more zealous soldiers of the faith, more loving communicants, more contrite penitents, more apostolic priests, and parents more united in Christ. Thus, in actual grace, the sacraments give us the power to do certain virtuous deeds which overcome the difficulties against our sacramental life and which fulfill the special purpose of each sacrament.

At the moment of Baptism, for example, the new Christian acquires a right to the actual graces proper to the first sacrament. If the newly baptized is an adult, he can receive such graces right away; if an infant, he will begin to receive his baptismal graces only after attaining the use of reason, when God first calls him to do his Christian duty. And for what special purpose does Baptism bestow its graces upon us? This sacrament gives us our first faith, and so the baptismal graces empower us to make acts of this virtue. Thus we overcome temptations against faith, we strengthen our faith, we are numbered among God's faithful. Through Baptism, moreover, we enter into God's family, the Catholic Church. Hence the graces of this sacrament will encourage and enable us to do those holy deeds which will keep us in the Church and increase our divine life as children of the Father.

Confirmation calls us to more active holiness and faith. It therefore brings us graces of action so that we can do those virtuous deeds which win from God increased vigor in our Christ-life and in our faith. Thus do God's children, though young in years, grow to supernatural manhood. The newly confirmed are now soldiers of God, ready to defend and to spread their Catholic faith—for to such an apostolate does Confirmation call them. Hence the graces of this sacrament arm them with courage and strength to fight the enemies of faith, to make their Church known, to explain their religion, to win converts and so to enlarge God's family here and hereafter.

Upon receiving the Holy Eucharist, we find our Savior in sacramental touch with our flesh. Wonderful as is such a nearness, it gives only a hint of the marvelous bond which the Blessed Sacrament effects between Christ and ourselves. For Holy Communion unites our souls to Jesus in a new, intimate, sacred, spiritual union, in a union of charity. Of course the other sacraments grant us charity—but as a help to one's grace of state, in order that the new Christian may be charitable to his brethren, that the penitent may hate his sins because they offend the infinitely lovable God, that the heart of the new priest may burn with love of God, that the Catholic husband may love his wife in Christ. The Holy Eucharist, however, brings us charity for the sake of charity, because charity is so valuable itself and so important in our divine life. Thus, charity is the constant companion of the grace that sanctifies; it includes the observance of God's Commandments; it enters into every holy deed; a sin against any other virtue is a sin against charity also; it is the greatest of virtues; it will eternally abide with us in Heaven.

And how does the Blessed Sacrament give us charity for its own sake? The moment we receive Communion, the Eucharistic Christ within our body grants us the sacramental graces of this holy rite—the graces of charity and union. Jesus Himself pours out His love upon us and in return begs our love; in the Sacrament of Love He thirsts for man's true love. So He generously grants us the actual graces of the Eucharist, with which He would make our souls alert and sensitive to His boundless love and through which He calls us into action, that is, to an active outpouring of our love for His Eucharistic Self. These sacramental graces are stirring graces, inspiring graces and strengthening graces. They arouse us to a greater love of Jesus; they increase our power to love Him; they encourage us to show Him a finer, purer love; they strengthen us to offer our Savior a love of affection, devotion and esteem; they inflame our souls with a burning love for Him; they enable us to make a generous consecration of our whole self to our sacra- mental God. Thus do the Eucharistic graces inspire and empower us to love of and union with Jesus within us; and if we use these graces, we shall offer to our sacramental Guest the holy outpouring of our full- hearted love. Then is the sacred purpose of the Eu- charist attained. For because we have received Him, Jesus especially loves us; and because His Eucharistic graces have enlarged our love for Him, we have, even after consuming the Blessed Sacrament, a loving union with Jesus through charity—and indeed, a closer union than before. Behold the mutual affection of God and man!

We said earlier that the sacramental graces help us to carry out the purpose of each sacrament. The aim of Penance is supernatural health—that is, the sanctity of our soul. Hence with the graces of this sacrament, we shall keep holy and grow holier, we shall preserve our divine life in an ever healthy condition. But this holy vitality man attains only by constant virtuous acts, which bespeak victory over the enemies of his soul. For our divine life is subject to crises. It can be attacked, even seriously, by disease from without and within: for instance, by temptations springing from the devil, the flesh, pride, lack of faith, greed, evil example and spiritual laziness. Moreover, man, by serious sin, can bring upon his supernatural life a mortal malady so that, unless he is cured, he stands at the door of eternal death in Hell.

Against such diseases Penance arms us with graces that are medicinal. These graces show the penitent what to do and inspire him to do it; in other words, to have contrition and to make reparation for his offenses. Futhermore, the penitential graces have power to heal the illnesses of our divine life. For in helping God's children to do the virtuous deeds proper to their Christian vocation, the graces of Penance serve as injections of confidence to the timid, faith to the prejudiced, courage to the faint-hearted, love to the proud, devotion to the hardened and zeal to the lazy. These injections last only a short time, yet long enough to enable us to perform those holy acts which weaken our evil habits, build up our powers for good (that is, our virtues), and enlarge our divine life. Again, the graces of this sacrament stir us to prayers of contrition. Thereby our faults are forgiven, the mortally diseased soul is cured in an instant, the sinner is brought back from the brink of eternal death in Hell and is restored to a full divine life. Lastly, the penitential graces are strengthening. While we are recuperating from a sick spell, we use a tonic and take exercise in order to prevent a relapse into further sickness, in order to build up our resistance against disease and death. Thus we shall recover the strength and the joy of good health. So too the penitent, using God's strong graces, performs deeds which are less selfish and more saintly; and through this holy exercise he lessens his evil inclinations and makes his habits of virtue vigorous. Thus will he enjoy a healthy soul-life here and hereafter.

Extreme Unction assists us through serious illnesses of the body and particularly through our final agony; it prepares us to face our divine Judge. Under the necessity of being at his spiritual best, the sick man needs the full use of his faculties. Yet he is sorely tried. Pain distracts his attention from godly things. His natural self is breaking up as death nears. The power of his mind and will is slowed down by his sick body. The help which such a one truly needs will come to him through the graces of Extreme Unction.

These graces will strengthen the sick man's soul for its struggle to reach Heaven. In his most important hour the sick person may be endangered by spiritual weakness. His past sins make him distrustful about his chances of entering Heaven; bodily pain weakens his will; under the attack of temptation, fear rises in his soul; he quails at the thought of his oncoming judgment. Here Extreme Unction brings to the anointed one healing graces, arousing graces—graces of peace and hope and power and perseverance, which supplant the sick person's worry and weakness with strength of will, a confident heart and peace of mind. With such help we can pray devoutly, receive Viaticum worthily, offer our love to God, persevere in holiness and accept death in union with our Savior's death. Thus does Extreme Unction help us to die in grace with God and man and prepare us for our new life in Heaven.

Holy Orders gives us priests who are called to father the divine life in all souls. This sacred purpose they seek to attain through works of zeal, through preaching and teaching, through the sacraments and the Holy Sacrifice of the Mass. Hence God's anointed receive many sacramental graces which enable them to carry on their priestly apostolate. With such help they offer Mass ever more devoutly; in pulpit and confessional they teach and guide souls; they bless the Catholic marriage of the faithful; young and old, sick and poor they serve generously; they lead their flock in prayer; they beget, protect, nourish and repair the divine life within the souls of their spiritual children. So do the graces of Holy Orders, while helping the priest to advance in the grace-life himself, enable him to carry on his sacred vocation as a father of God's family.

The purpose of Matrimony is to bind the family together in a sacred supernatural union. The Catholic bride and groom are wed within the sanctuary, where they seal their union by receiving together the one Lord of all. The graces which Matrimony brings them are the graces of vocation—of their calling to be spouses and parents in Christ. Thereby God enables man and wife to support and comfort each other, to love one another ever more surely, to bear with each other's defects and to continue their married life as a life of holiness. With the sacramental graces, moreover, husband and wife fulfill God's law within the family. Gladly they offer themselves to the tasks of family life. Guarding their purity, they remain faithful to each other so that in union they can carry out the works of their vocation. They labor obediently to bring forth children and to rear them in the Catholic way. They take care that their little ones receive and nourish the divine life of their own souls through prayer and the sacraments. They train their young to obey and to be kind, at the same time giving them holy example—through acts of faith, courage, prayer, temperance and charity. So do the matrimonial graces help the Catholic husband and wife to carry on the duties of their married state, to grow in the divine life together, and to make of themselves and their children a holy family in Christ.

CHAPTER FOURTEEN : *A Life of Sonship*

I

Gᴏᴅ is the master of life; He lays down its laws. Only
He can make life from nothing; in every birth He plays
the principal part. From God come all the different
kinds of life; and once He puts it into being, life passes
on through generation alone. That is a law of life with
which only God, the Law-maker, can interfere—as He
did when His Son, taking a human body, was neither
conceived nor born as are other men. Yet the law remains that life is passed on only through generation. God
made the first tree; that tree, producing seed, begets
other trees in kind. The same holds true of the grace-life
which adorns our souls. That heavenly life, in Christ's
plan for the New Testament, first becomes ours by
generation and that is the ordinary law of divine life for
us.

Sometimes people speak of men as born Catholics.
That is really not true; there are no born Catholics. Had

Adam not sinned, his children would have been born friends of God, but the first sin lost for us this happy birthright. So man today is not born possessing the divine life, a member of the Catholic Church. On the contrary, we are born and conceived in the state of sin.

Such is our first coming to life, our birth in the flesh as children of men. We are begotten of our human parents and the fruit of their labor is a child, born in original sin. When men held others as slaves, the offspring of slaves were born into slavery; we, born in sin, are born slaves of sin. "For . . . you were the servants of sin." [106] But we have been redeemed from sin by Christ and through Him we enjoy a second birth into a higher life. This rebirth does not come "of blood nor of the will of the flesh nor of the will of man," [107] since that is a birth into sin. Rather, men's regeneration occurs only when they "are born of God"; [108] that is the true law of life for all men of the New Testament.

Our second birth takes place at Baptism, when a man is "born again of water and the Holy Ghost." [109] As Mary by the power of the Holy Spirit [110] brought forth Jesus, so water by the power of the Holy Ghost begets other Christs. On Holy Saturday when she blesses the baptismal font, the Church through her priest prays: "May the virtue of the Holy Ghost descend into all the water of this font and make the whole substance of this water fruitful for regeneration." The fruit of Baptism is

[106] Rom. 6:20.
[107] John 1:13.
[108] John 1:13.
[109] John 3:5.
[110] Luke 1:35.

regeneration, our second birth whereby we are born again to our new life. Listen once more to the Church's prayer on Holy Saturday: "And may that same Holy Spirit by the hidden virtue of His Godhead make fruitful this water prepared for the regeneration of men, that a heavenly offspring, conceived in sanctification, may emerge from the immaculate womb of this divine font, reborn to newness of life." Through water and the Holy Ghost we are born of God, "a heavenly offspring." He who by his first birth is a child of man, is by his second birth a child of God. "For of his own will hath he begotten us." [111] At Our Lord's baptism "the Holy Ghost descended . . . as a dove upon him" [112] and the Father said: "This is my beloved Son in whom I am well pleased." [113] At our baptism God the Father can rightly call us His beloved sons, while "the Spirit himself giveth testimony to our spirit that we are the sons of God." [114] As the Blessed Virgin, beholding her newborn Child, realized that now the Son of God was also the Son of Man, so the Catholic mother, embracing her newly baptized infant, can rejoice that now the son of her womb is also the son of God.

Of course we are not sons of God in the way Our Lord is. He is the Father's Son in every true sense; we are God's adopted children. "God sent his Son . . . that we might receive the adoption of sons." [115] Adoption means the accepting of a person, not born of oneself, as

[111] James 1:18.
[112] Luke 3:22.
[113] Matt. 3:17.
[114] Rom. 8:16.
[115] Gal. 4:4–5.

one's own child. Thus, when Pharao's daughter took to herself the young Moses, Scripture says "she adopted him for a son." [116] The adopted person is received as a son—with the rights of a son to share his new parents' love, table, home and goods. We admire a man who adopts an orphan child; yet God's adoption of us through the grace of Baptism far surpasses human adoption.

For example, men usually adopt because, lacking a child of their own, they yearn for the love of a little one; God adopts, not needing us at all but out of His boundless love for us, that we may be images of His Son, Jesus. Again, we adopt as sons, not animals but the children of men; for adoption demands that the one adopted be a man like his new parents. As merely human, then, we could not be sons of the Father. Hence God through sanctifying grace gives us a higher nature and lifts us to a life somehow divine so that He can adopt us as His sons. Lastly, no man adopts the child whom he has himself fathered; God's adoption includes our birth from Him through Baptism, so that He is our Father. "Behold what manner of love the Father has bestowed upon us, that we should be called children of God: and such we are . . . Beloved, now we are the children of God." [117]

But if all who live the divine life are children of the Father, then we must—and do—form under God one large family. Speakers sometimes talk about a brotherhood of man under the fatherhood of God as if such a union could spring from merely human toil. Yet God can be our Father and all mankind brothers only on the level

[116] Exod. 2:10.
[117] I John 3:1–2 (Confraternity of Christian Doctrine version).

of grace and holiness. Humanly speaking, men are by creation God's handiwork—and nothing more! Only through Baptism are we born of the one Father, raised to the divine childhood and made members of God's family.

Such is the heavenly brotherhood to which God gives all men a vocation, a call. This union is "the household of the faith," [118] in which we are "members of God's household," [119] that is, not servants but children at home in God's family. Thus souls living the life of grace, since they were born of the same Father, become indeed brothers and sisters. So St. Peter calls St. Paul "our most dear brother," [120] while the latter calls Appia "our dearest sister." [121] Again St. Paul speaks of Sosthenes as "a brother" [122] and of a Christian woman as "a sister." [123] Moreover, he often addresses the faithful as "brethren," [124] "my brethren," [125] "the brethren who are with me" [126] and "the brethren in the Lord." [127] These same words, used by the Church nineteen centuries ago, the priest of today still uses. When preaching to his parishioners, he calls them "my dear brethren." Let us love to be saluted as brethren. Our priest does not call us "ladies and gentlemen" or even "friends" but "dear brethren." We can be gentlemen and friends while being mere men; we are brethren only when born of God.

[118] Gal. 6:10.
[119] Eph. 2:19 (Confraternity of Christian Doctrine version).
[120] II Peter 3:15.
[121] Philemon 2.
[122] I Cor. 1:1.
[123] I Cor. 9:5.
[124] Rom. 1:13; I Cor. 2:1.
[125] Rom. 7:4; I Cor. 1:11.
[126] Phil. 4:22.
[127] Phil. 1:14.

If this were all our divine brotherhood meant, it would be glorious indeed. However, not only did God the Father beget us through Baptism; He also begot from eternity God the Son, who became Christ our Savior. Thus Jesus is the first-born Son of God the Father and we, other children of the same Father, are His brothers. To Margaret of Cortona, great sinner and greater saint, Our Lord once said: "Remember that you are My slave by your sins but My sister through your state of grace." Yes, Jesus is our older Brother, "the first-born amongst many brethren," [128] and through Him souls in grace become brothers and sisters of each other. Have we not truly entered a divine family, we who are children of God the Father and brothers of God the Son! The world's leaders cry for union and they do unite some men in trade, arms, labor, culture and education. Yet these bonds avail little unless there exists also the divine brotherhood of souls in Christ, which influences all other human ties.

II

Adam, we read, "begot a son to his own image and likeness." [129] That a parent should beget young like himself is the very heart of generation; for parents do not make children from materials outside themselves as a sculptor makes a statue, but in begetting they give their young something of their own living selves. Hence children bear a likeness to their parents, so that between

[128] Rom. 8:29.
[129] Gen. 5:3.

them there often exists a strong family likeness. We are truly the living images of our parents.

Thus we note the important part that likeness plays in generation. Our heavenly Father begot from eternity God the Son. Where is the likeness between them? God the Son, Our Lord, is the living image of His Father. "Christ . . . is the image of God"; [130] He "is the image of the invisible God." [131] Human parents bear a child by giving him a human nature; God the Father begot His Son by giving Him a divine nature, not another divine nature like the Father's but the one identical divine nature which the Father Himself has. For this reason the Son is a perfect likeness of His Father.

But we, too, souls living the life of grace, were born of God in Baptism. Where, then, can be found the likeness between us and our divine Parent? The likeness lies in this, that by our baptism God gives us a nature like His own, a nature somehow divine, since all birth means the passing on of a nature like that of the parents. So God the Father gave His First-born the divine nature; so to us, His younger sons, He has given a divine nature. True, the Son possesses the one divine nature of the Godhead, whereas we are said to share the divine nature; yet precisely in that partaking of the divine nature consists the likeness between souls born to grace and their heavenly Parent.

As children of God, then, we share His divine nature. "He hath given us most great and precious promises: that by these you may be made partakers of the divine

[130] II Cor. 4:4.
[131] Col. 1:15.

nature." [132] We know how a child possesses his parents' nature, but how do we partake of God's nature? Holy persons partake in the sense that they possess something like the divine nature. The part of man most like God takes on a likeness of God's nature; that is, our soul through Baptism receives a real spiritual gift which makes it like to God. The wondrous gift we speak of is sanctifying grace.

And how does sanctifying grace make us sharers of the divine nature? The grace of holiness is a gift above all other created gifts, a gift of a divine order. Hence it raises the soul to a divine level of being. Sanctifying grace, while allowing us to remain ourselves, is a new and higher nature within us. It adds to our human being a godlike nature—an inward source of divine life and power. It makes of us a new creature, most closely approaching the divine and so lofty that God describes us as sharing His own divine nature.

By God's favor His grace within our soul makes us partake of His very being; the grace of holiness lets us share in God's perfection. Thus sanctifying grace gives us:

1. a divine life, for through the baptismal grace we are born sons of God, living the life of our Parent;
2. a divine holiness, for sanctifying grace is the holiness most like God's;
3. divine power, for this grace empowers us to do deeds worthy of a divine reward;
4. divine knowledge, for, with the faith which accompanies sanctifying grace into our soul, we

[132] II Peter 1:4.

know truths which were known only to God till
Christ revealed them;

5. a divine will, for, when we have the grace of holi-
    ness, our will is to do God's will;

6. divine virtue, for sanctified souls in their charity
    love as God does;

7. divine work, for holy persons have a vocation to
    work for God's cause;

8. divine dignity, for souls in grace are worthy to be
    called sons of God and to receive the divine food
    of the Eucharist at the Lord's table.

9. a divine home, for Heaven, God's home, is the
    birthright of those who live in sanctifying grace.

So in grace men do possess a gift which is somehow
divine, men do share in God's perfection. Moreover,
sanctifying grace is rightly considered a nature because
it is the inmost source of all our actions as children of
God—of all our supernatural life and holiness and
strength and value. Rightly then can we claim that
sanctifying grace adds to our manhood a godlike nature,
a share of the divine nature.

It will help now to sum up all we have said. Where is
the likeness between God and the children He fathered
in Baptism? In this, that by our sacramental birth we
share in God's very nature. It is sanctifying grace in our
souls that makes us partake of the divine nature. For
sanctifying grace is the inmost source of our divine life
and action. Hence with right we call it a share of God's
own being, perfection, nature. In the grace of holiness,
therefore, consists the family likeness between God and

His saintly children. And who better than God's own sons should possess His divine nature!

III

At the Annunciation Gabriel told Our Lady: "The Holy which shall be born of thee shall be called the Son of God." [133] Something like this happens at our sacramental birth, for it is the soul precisely as holy which God begets through Baptism. By the power of the Holy Spirit water washes the soul of sin, pours into it divine holiness and floods it with the life of God's own child. Thereby we enjoy a divine life and holiness. "Whosoever is born of God committeth not sin: for his seed abideth in him and he can not sin, because he is born of God." [134] The newly baptized resembles God, in whom life and holiness are one, who possesses no life which is not at the same time holy. Moreover, because of his baptismal innocence he shares in the perfection of God's nature and carries on the family trait of our divine Parent.

The gift of divine life and holiness we call sanctifying grace. It is the grace of life and the life of grace. It is our holiness, our life as children of God. It is the foundation of our virtues and the root of all holy living. It makes our good deeds divinely holy in themselves and worthy of life eternal. It grows with our every act of virtue. It is the holiness of the New Testament and for us there is no other holiness. Into such sanctity does Baptism beget us.

[133] Luke 1:35.
[134] I John 3:9.

Born to divine life and sonship, we are born as well to divine holiness.

No wonder God honors His faithful children with such holy titles. They are "the beloved of God, called to be saints." [135] As long as they live the divine life, they are "the elect of God, holy and beloved." [136] They are "fellow citizens with the saints," [137] each one a "saint in Christ Jesus." [138] Through St. Paul God often calls His holy ones saints, while that Apostle labels himself "the least of all the saints." [139] We limit the word "saint" to the Church's canonized saints, but for Paul a saint meant a Christian who through Baptism has been consecrated to God and who remains faithfully holy as befits a person so consecrated. Souls in grace are "a people acceptable, a pursuer of good works" [140] and even in Heaven "they are numbered among the children of God and their lot is among the saints." [141]

Moreover, we who nourish the life of grace and sonship are "the household of the faith," [142] "planted in the house of the Lord." [143] No matter how lowly, we stand before men "a chosen generation, a kingly priesthood, a holy nation, a purchased people." [144] United, we form "the people of God," [145] "the city of the living God." [146]

[135] Rom. 1:7.
[136] Col. 3:12.
[137] Eph. 2:19.
[138] Phil. 4:21.
[139] Eph. 3:8.
[140] Titus 2:14.
[141] Wisd. 5:5.
[142] Gal. 6:10.
[143] Psalm 91:14.
[144] I Peter 2:9.
[145] Heb. 4:9; 11:25.
[146] Heb. 12:22.

In our sanctity we are "the temple of God": "for the temple of God is holy, which you are." [147] Lastly, we make up "the kingdom of God," [148] "the kingdom of Heaven" [149] on earth.

Sanctity is nearness to God. Jesus and Mary are most holy because they are nearest to God. Is the soul in grace holy in this way? Look at the titles we have just recounted and see if God shows Himself therein.

First, sanctity means that man is free from mortal sin, a "saint in Christ Jesus." Secondly, by sanctity we mean a soul adorned with virtue, worthy to be "the temple of God." Then, too, saintliness supposes that our will is directed toward God, that we are set in godliness, that we seek God in our deeds, that we are "the people of God." Moreover, by our baptismal holiness we became "the children of God"—a family set apart from the pagan world and consecrated to the worship, love and obedience of God. Again, sanctity means our union with God. For a Catholic, holiness means union with the indwelling God, who in a special way makes Himself at home within our soul and there abides as long as we possess sanctifying grace. In this union the Triune God gives Himself to us and we give ourselves to Him; God lives in us and we live our divine life in Him; through His graces God keeps in touch with our mind and will, while we through prayer and other virtuous deeds keep in touch with God. So the union of God with holy souls is the union of one friend with another, of a father with his children, in "the kingdom of God." Finally, because we

[147] I Cor. 3:16–17.
[148] Matt. 12:28; Luke 10:9–11.
[149] Matt. 5:19; 16:19.

are holy, our will loves God above all other things. In turn we become dear to God, the objects of His boundless love, "the beloved of God." Thus we see how the name of God is connected with His holy ones and how they are linked with Him. Sanctity is indeed nearness to God! His children, born to holiness and faithful to that vocation, are really very near and dear to God!

IV

A boy remains the child of his father always. Never may he rightly deny his parents; even in the next world he is their flesh and blood eternally. We likewise, who were born of the Father, may never deny our divine sonship. No matter what our age and rank before men, we are God's children forever.

In the human family a day comes when the young outgrow their parental home. We never outgrow God's family; to live in it forever is our duty, vocation and glory as God's children. God could have brought us to holiness while leaving us His servants—which we would be as mere creatures—but He willed to make us holy by making us His own sons. We need not have been sons in order to be holy; now we do. In fact, our divine sonship is the foundation of our spiritual life, for we begin that life only by being born sons of the Father. Know it or not, we live our grace-life only by living as God's faithful children.

Yet men are not always devoted sons of God. The prodigal son confessed to his father, "I have sinned against Heaven and before thee. I am not now worthy to be called thy son." [150] The Catholic in mortal sin is likewise unworthy to call God his Father. The terrible crime of Judas caused our Savior to say: "It were better for him if that man had not been born." [151] Jesus regretted ever having made this Apostle. We do not want any sin of ours to make God regret having begotten us in Baptism. So many Catholics, however, seem not to know or appreciate their divine sonship. As our parents' children, we love our name, we strive to bring honor to it, we work to further the good reputation of our family. Similarly God the Father wants us to live a life worthy of our birthright as His sons; He wants us never to disgrace the divine family, whose saintly members are our kinsfolk in Christ. "For whosoever shall do the will of God, he is my brother and my sister and mother." [152] The sinful Catholic can "be compared to a man beholding his own countenance in a glass. For he beheld himself and went his way and presently forgot what manner of man he was." [153] Even if the world does not see in us God's own children, let us never forget what manner of men we are—that is, men born to a life divine as sons of the Father.

Hence, as men of God, we must live up to our divine sonship. Our baptism was a birth "not of blood nor of the will of the flesh nor of the will of man"; [154] we were not born of God according to sin or according to the flesh. So we are called to overcome mortal sin all our

[150] Luke 15:21.
[151] Mark 14:21.
[152] Mark 3:35.
[153] James 1:23–24.
[154] John 1:13.

days. Moreover, we may not live only for the flesh. "Not in bread alone doth man live." [155] No, the members of God's household may not live merely for food, drink, fashionable clothing, bodily comfort and the pleasures of the flesh; neither should we glory in mere fleshly beauty or strength. "For if you live according to the flesh, you shall die." [156] Shortly before Jacinta of Fatima died, the Blessed Mother appeared to her, looking very sad, and told the child the reason for her sorrow: "The sins that bring most souls to hell are the sins of the flesh." [157] St. Paul, who well knew this danger of eternal death, gives us his remedy: "I chastise my body and bring it into subjection: lest . . . I myself should become a castaway." [158]

Our question, then, reads: As God's own children, how should we live? How should we act so as to continue worthy of our divine sonship? We shall be wise if we learn how the first Son of God was devoted to and united with the eternal Father who begot Him.

Jesus mirrored His Father: "He that seeth me seeth the Father also." [159] The Son of God mirrored His Father's thoughts; He taught what His Father commanded Him to teach: "The words which thou gavest me, I have given to them." [160] Our Lord's will was not His own but the Father's: "Not my will but thine be done." [161] His desires mirrored His Father's desires: "I

[155] Matt. 4:4.
[156] Rom. 8:13.
[157] De Marchi, *The Crusade of Fatima*, p. 137.
[158] I Cor. 9:27.
[159] John 14:9.
[160] John 17:8.
[161] Luke 22:42.

do always the things that please him." [162] Continually our Savior's mind turned to the Father; often He raised His Sacred Heart to His Father in prayer, especially during the Passion: "Father, forgive them . . . Father, into thy hands I commend my spirit." [163] Always Jesus labored "about my Father's business"; [164] always He toiled to glorify His Father: "I honor my Father"; [165] "I have glorified thee on the earth . . . I have manifested thy name." [166] Our Lord loved His Father with the love of a Son who was God: "I love the Father"; [167] in turn He was loved by the Father with an eternal love: "The Father loveth the Son." [168]

Thus we see how devoted Christ was to the Father; in fact, devotion to His Father was the very heart of Our Lord's holiness. The Son of God took flesh in order to teach us by His deeds how sons of God, who are human beings, should live. "I have given you an example that as I have done to you, so you do also." [169] For, being children of the Father, we have a duty to live as did the first-born Son of God. How then do we show devotion to our divine Father after our Savior's example? The child of God obeys his heavenly Father. "Moreover, we have had fathers of our flesh for instructors and we reverenced them: shall we not much more obey the Father of spirits and live?" [170] The good Catholic keeps

[162] John 8:29.
[163] Luke 23:34, 46.
[164] Luke 2:49.
[165] John 8:49.
[166] John 17:4, 6.
[167] John 14:31.
[168] John 3:35.
[169] John 13:15.
[170] Heb. 12:9.

the Commandments; he must, if he wants the Father to love him. "If anyone love me, he will keep my word and my Father will love him." [171] A son of God prays to his Father in the very phrases Jesus gave us: "Our Father, who art in Heaven." [172] The holy soul, furthermore, fasts joyfully and gives alms unselfishly; and because he does, the "Father, who seeth in secret, will repay thee." [173] Again, taught by Our Lord to pray "forgive us our trespasses," the baptized person forgives his persecutors. "For if you will forgive men their offences, your heavenly Father will forgive you also your offences." [174] In the face of suffering the sanctified soul embraces his Father's will: "Not my will but thine be done." [175] With Christ, furthermore, the child of God loves his divine Father: "I love the Father." [176] With that same Father the Catholic loves his Savior in brotherly devotion; hence the Father loves him as He does His Son Jesus: "Thou hast . . . loved them as thou hast also loved me." [177] Then too the faithful soul loves his neighbors as kinsmen in Christ: "This is my commandment, that you love one another as I have loved you." [178]

Thus do we seek to carry on Our Lord's devotion to His Father and ours. Thus do we aim to be "perfect as also your heavenly Father is perfect." [179] Thus do we

[171] John 14:23.
[172] Matt. 6:9–13.
[173] Matt. 6:4, 18.
[174] Matt. 6:14.
[175] Luke 22:42.
[176] John 14:31.
[177] John 17:23.
[178] John 15:12.
[179] Matt. 5:48.

labor to grow in our divine sonship. Thus do we glorify the Father. "In this is my Father glorified, that you bring forth very much fruit." [180] Furthermore, by the example of our virtue we glorify God before our fellow men. "So let your light shine before men that they may see your good works and glorify your Father who is in Heaven." [181] Briefly, our life of holiness is spent with Christ to the honor and glory of the Father for ever and ever. In this way we live the divine life as devout sons of God; in this way are we always worthy to call God, the Father of Jesus, our own dear Father too.

V

A child who has attained the full use of reason is facing his first temptation to sin mortally. That child has either been baptized or not. To overcome his temptation the unbaptized youngster receives the help of God called actual grace. The baptized youngster already possesses his first share of sanctifying grace; and to strengthen him further against temptation God will give actual grace to him also. Each boy received grace—the unbaptized, actual; and the baptized, sanctifying. The boys could not do for God any deeds that would earn these graces. Of themselves they did not deserve grace. For them grace was a pure gift, given out of God's goodness. Certainly the unbaptized boy of his own power could do nothing that would merit grace from God, while the baptized boy received the grace of holiness as a helpless babe.

Now let us suppose that these boys, using grace well,

[180] John 15:8.
[181] Matt. 5:16.

proceed through future graces to advance in holiness all their days. On their early graces the youngsters have built a spiritual temple of persevering virtue and sanctity. Yet that entire structure of lifelong holiness, because it is founded on the free grace of God, is itself a divine gift. In this sense even the Heaven which comes at the end of a virtuous life is due to God's loving gift of His first grace. This is true whether we reach life eternal by preserving our baptismal innocence till death or whether we die in holiness only after bewailing our mortal sins. Hence St. Paul can say that salvation will be ours through the mercy of God: "According to his mercy he saved us." [182] God "hath delivered and called us . . . according to his own purpose and grace." [183] Again, the Apostle tells us plainly that we shall receive Heaven as a gift of God. "For the wages of sin is death. But the grace of God, life everlasting." [184]

Nevertheless, though Heaven remains God's gracious gift, we can still lay some claim to it. We are the children of God; and "unless you become as little children, you shall not enter into the kingdom of Heaven." [185] But as among men children fall heir to their parents' goods, so God's children are heirs to His goods, to life eternal: "If a son, an heir also through God." [186] Hence Heaven is our fatherland. It is our true home, the kingdom of our Father. With Jesus we can call it "My Father's house." [187]

[182] Titus 3:5.
[183] II Tim. 1:9.
[184] Rom. 6:23.
[185] Matt. 18:3.
[186] Gal. 4:7.
[187] John 14:2.

Thither through His Ascension Christ, our older Brother, leads the children of inheritance to God the Father. Even for our Blessed Mother Heaven means life eternal with the Father, her Father too.

Thus Heaven is a patrimony which we claim because of our divine sonship. So do baptized infants, dying before the age of reason, inherit Heaven as heirs of life eternal. Yet, like the prodigal son,[188] we can waste our inheritance on riotous living. Our claim to blessedness will not be honored if we die disobedient children of the Father. "For you know this . . . that no fornicator or unclean or covetous person . . . hath inheritance in the kingdom . . . of God." [189] Only by remaining devoted sons of the Father shall we obtain Heaven as our birthright. Moreover, because even on earth we belong to the divine family, we should confidently hope for the eternal life promised to us by our Father. "Justified by his grace, we may be heirs according to hope of life everlasting. It is a faithful saying." [190] We, who are graced with holiness, can hope for life everlasting as our inheritance; and that hope of His children God will uphold faithfully.

But if God fulfills the hope of His dear ones in the next world, He has already pledged our inheritance here. Even before their parents' death children truly enjoy part of their inheritance, for instance, the family's good name and the benefits of wealth. In the same way God the Father lets us begin on earth to enjoy our heavenly birthright. We have started life eternal by living the

[188] Luke 15:13.
[189] Eph. 5:5.
[190] Titus 3:7–8.

divine life of grace, by receiving from Christ the truths of faith, by sharing God's perfections, by loving God through charity, by commencing our eternal companion-ship with Jesus and Mary and the saints. Yet besides helping us to begin our Heaven now, God, as far as He is concerned, also pledges our future inheritance. This He does through His gift of the Blessed Trinity dwelling within us. To the Holy Ghost, the Spirit of love, is particularly assigned the work of sealing our heavenly heritage because for God it is a labor of love. The Holy Spirit "is the pledge of our inheritance." [191]

St. Paul took that word "pledge" from the market place. On the lips of merchants in the Apostle's day a pledge meant the first down-payment on a sale, given in token that the entire debt will be paid later. Men today also make such down-payments as a pledge that they in time will pay the full amount of their purchase. So too does God, whose children we are, give us a pledge of our divine inheritance—a pledge we could never have as mere men—the Holy Spirit living within our souls in dearest friendship. We shall possess God face to face in Heaven; through grace we possess in a special way our divine Friend, the Spirit of love and promise. Thus the Holy Ghost dwelling within us is a foretaste and first share of the heavenly heritage which will be ours. God "hath sealed us and given the pledge of the Spirit in our hearts." [192] Lovers give and receive an engagement ring in token that the full gift of themselves to each other will be given later. The Holy Spirit is the pledge be-

[191] Eph. 1:14.
[192] II Cor. 1:22.

tween God and man, giving us a strong hope of enjoying our full birthright in Heaven.

But how does the Holy Spirit pledge our inheritance? He "giveth testimony . . . that we are the sons of God. And if sons, heirs also: heirs indeed of God and joint heirs with Christ." [193] The Holy Ghost bears witness that with Jesus we are sons and heirs of God. "And because you are sons, God hath sent the Spirit of his Son into your hearts, crying: Abba, Father." [194] See how intimately God's child here lives with the three divine Persons! Moreover, the Holy Ghost labors to increase our holiness, for only the holy may be heirs of God. Thereby the Holy Spirit makes our soul like Himself, a holy spirit which can call Heaven its home. Again, the Holy Ghost is the bond of love between God and ourselves; in Him, as do the Father and the Son, God and saintly men love each other. Such abiding charity leads us surely to "an inheritance incorruptible . . . reserved in Heaven for you." [195] Our holiness, lastly, includes gifts that can remain forever (charity), and those that do not (faith and hope). As long as the Holy Spirit dwells within us, He is God's guarantee to His sons that faith will yield to the direct sight of God, and hope to gladness unending. Thus does God through the Spirit of love put the divine seal on our soul, claim it as His own, rejoice to live in it and pledge Himself to it as its birthright forever.

Yet not alone by right of sonship do we enter our

[193] Rom. 8:16 and 17.
[194] Gal. 4:6.
[195] I Peter 1:4.

fatherland; God lets us claim it also by way of reward. "Your reward is very great in Heaven." [196] The divine plan calls those with the use of reason to win Heaven by their own toil; no longer may they claim the home of the blessed merely as their birthright. A man's eternal destiny, once he reaches the age of reason, will be either Heaven or Hell—"according as he hath done, whether it be good or evil." [197] Hence we must earn Heaven by holy deeds; that is our task here, the warfare of life, the labor of love for God's children. "Be thou faithful unto death: and I will give thee the crown of life." [198] By heeding the Commandments, by defeating serious temptations, by caring for the duties of their state, by every virtuous deed persons in sanctifying grace earn their heavenly reward. "For God is not unjust, that he should forget your work and the love which you have shown in his name." [199] Thus we who live the divine life can by our holy actions win eternal happiness. At the Last Judgment Christ will call [200] the blessed to enjoy His Father's kingdom because of their merciful deeds. St. Paul, moreover, tells us that our brief trial here "worketh for us above measure exceedingly an eternal weight of glory." [201] Such value shines forth in the good deeds of saintly men!

Of course God through His grace plays by far the greater part in each holy act we do; furthermore, He

[196] Matt. 5:12.
[197] II Cor. 5:10.
[198] Apoc. 2:10.
[199] Heb. 6:10.
[200] Matt. 25:34ff.
[201] II Cor. 4:17.

lets us claim as our merit what He so largely does. Yet our part, tiny as compared with God's, is so valuable that on it can depend our Heaven—or Hell. For in all holy deeds we do choose to act rightly when we could at the same time decide to sin. "And every man shall receive his own reward according to his own labor." [202] Hence adults who die in God's favor claim Heaven by a double title: their birthright and their reward. Indeed, God honors His children by letting them merit life eternal. For to earn Heaven is greater than merely to inherit it; again, merit brings us a richer blessedness in Heaven. Our acts of love for, and devotion to, God and man increase the grace of holiness within us and that grace measures our eternal joy in the Father's kingdom.

So we see that God offers us His heavenly home as a pure gift. Then too we can claim it for our birthright because we were born sons of God with a right to our Father's goods. That baptismal birth, however, was also a divine gift in no way deserved. Lastly, we merit Heaven—yet only because God deigns to reckon deeds done with His grace as worthy of winning for us eternal glory. We enter Heaven with some claim to earning it, with some claim to inheriting it—but always and foremost it remains the gift of God's generous love to men.

VI

Human life became ours through the work of a mother and a father. We took on the grace-life by being born of God alone, for He is so powerful that He begets

[202] I Cor. 3:8.

souls to the divine life without any helpmate. Yet the Father, knowing His children's ways, saw that in living their divine life they would need a mother also. Hence He gave us for our spiritual Mother Mary, the Mother of His own first-born Son and our elder Brother, Jesus.

But why may we call Mary our Mother? Mary conceived of the Holy Ghost; she bore in her womb a Child; she shared her flesh with Him; in the fulness of time she gave birth to Him who was named the Christ. Mary mothered a man—yet not merely a man. The Person she mothered is the Son of God in human flesh, God who took from Mary a human body, God made man. Moreover, Mary's work in bearing her Child far surpassed the labor of all other mothers. Suppose a babe just born will someday be his country's hero. His mother begets him, not as a hero, but only as a child whose future she knows not. Mary, however, gave birth to her Son as the Savior of men. From His first moment, Jesus was the Redeemer and acted to redeem us; from His first instant within Mary's womb, Jesus knew He was the Savior and gladly did the Savior's work. "And she shall bring forth a son and thou shalt call his name Jesus. For he shall save his people from their sins." [203] There was not a second of His life when Jesus failed to be our Redeemer; even in His Mother's body He did His saving work for us. Again, the name "Jesus" which God "gave him before he was conceived in the womb" [204] shows why He took flesh of Mary—to save men from the slavery of sin. Truly "there is no other name under Heaven given to

[203] Matt. 1:21.
[204] Luke 2:21.

men whereby we must be saved." [205] Hence Jesus—and no one else unless through Him—is the Savior of men's souls; and He saves us, not as God alone, but as God made man in and through the flesh Mary gave Him. Thus did Mary mother Him precisely as our Savior.

By redeeming us Jesus won for all men the forgiveness of sins and the grace of holiness. He is the Life of the world, and Our Lady bore Him as the Life. He came among us that we might "have life and . . . have it more abundantly." [206] "In him was life" [207]—the life of sanctifying grace included, the life He shares with us in His mystical Self. The full Christ is indeed the mystic Christ and so, writes St. Augustine, the Mother of Jesus in the flesh is the Mother of His Mystical Body also. "She is clearly the spiritual Mother of His members which we are: because she co-operated by her charity that the faithful might be born into the Church; and these are the members of the same Head." [208] Mary, by mothering the Life, mothers those who through grace share the life; like a true mother, she gives us life, the grace-life, the Christ-life. No wonder that in the prayer "Hail, Holy Queen" the Church calls Mother Mary "our life"!

Let us put this same thought in another way. Jesus, our Savior and Life, is officially Head of the Mystical Body—and that from His first instant in Mary's body. "Within her virginal womb Christ Our Lord already bore the exalted title of Head of the Church; in a marvel-

[205] Acts 4:12.
[206] John 10:10.
[207] John 1:4.
[208] St. Augustine, *De Sancta Virginitate*, Chap. VI.

127

ous birth she brought Him forth as source of all supernatural life." [209] Mary conceived and bore Jesus precisely
as the Head of His Mystic Body; and since we are part
of that Body, Mary becomes our Mother also. On this
point St. Louis de Montfort, the apostle of devotion to
Our Lady, speaks. "One and the same mother does not
bring forth into the world the head without the members or the members without the head; for this would be
a monster of nature. So in like manner, in the order of
grace the Head and the members are born of one and the
same Mother." [210] Thus Mary becomes the Mother of all
who "have been baptized in Christ, have put on
Christ" [211] and are made one with Him in His Church.

But how does Mary mother us "in the order of
grace"? God planned that Mary play a part in our redemption next to her Son's. The actual birth of the
Savior depended on Mary's free choice to be His Mother.
She gave Him the Precious Blood He shed for us at His
Circumcision; she gave Him the life He offered for us
on Calvary; and all the days between, she centered her
love and devotion on the Savior and His task of saving
men. Moreover, God's plan for Mary's partnership in
our redemption called her to be the Mother, not of Jesus
alone, but of all men. That Marian motherhood of men
finds its source in the Annunciation and Incarnation. By
mothering Jesus as the Head of His Mystic Body, Mary
becomes the Mother of that Body also. In the years that
follow she readies herself to take a mother's care of her

[209] Pius XII, Encyclical *Mystici Corporis Christi*, June 29, 1943.
[210] De Montfort, *True Devotion to the Blessed Virgin*, n. 32.
[211] Gal. 3:27.

children. She lives a life of pain and sacrifice, that her
prayers may have more weight with her Son in winning
for us the graces of holiness. Indeed, by the sword of
sorrow suffered in our behalf she deserves to be again
called our Mother. "Thus she who corporally was the
Mother of our Head, through the added title of pain and
glory became spiritually the Mother of all His members." [212] Then at the chosen moment the Mystical Body
"was born from the side of our Savior on the Cross." [213]
Jesus by dying won for us the graces which make men
His brothers and members of His Mystical Body. Mary
too plays her part in our redemption. With the sorrow-
ful love of a mother's heart she offers her Son to the
Father and after His death starts to mother His new
brothers, the members of His new Mystical Body. At
the Annunciation Mary became the Mother of men; on
Calvary Jesus gave her His new brothers and sisters as
her own children forevermore. From the Annunciation
to Calvary Mary waited for these holy people, her new
sons and daughters; now in God's family she has, besides
Jesus, other children on whom she can lavish a mother's
love.

Nor was Our Lady slow to take up her motherly tasks
for those whom the risen Christ called [214] His brethren,
the children of grace who henceforth would be her
spiritual family. By her prayer she won for us the descent of the Holy Ghost upon the Church. "She it was
who, through her powerful prayers, obtained the grace

[212] Encyclical *Mystici Corporis Christi.*
[213] *Ibid.*
[214] John 20:17.

that the Spirit of our divine Redeemer . . . should be bestowed through miraculous gifts on the newly founded hierarchy on Pentecost." [215] Throughout her earthly life Mary cared for the growing Body of her Son with motherly devotion: "She continued to show for the Mystical Body of Christ . . . the same mother's care and ardent love with which she clasped the Infant Jesus to her warm and nourishing breast." [216]

Even after her Assumption into Heaven Mary remains our Mother and showers on us a mother's affection. God gave her, under Christ, a part in our redemption. Through the centuries, then, Mary in Heaven works to keep us, other Christs, as her devoted children and to ensure our salvation. Hence she begs for us the one important help to eternal life, the grace of God; indeed, no grace comes to men unless Mary first begs it for us from her Son. "Therefore truly and properly may we assert that by God's wish nothing at all of that enormous treasure of grace won by Our Lord is distributed to us except through Mary." [217] By her intercession Our Lady acquires for us the graces of holiness and action with which she arms her children to defeat the devil in all his temptations, gives us every help we need to live and die virtuously, and forms in our souls the life and holiness of her Son, so that the one Christ-life flourishes in Jesus and in her other children. So does Mary see Christ in all graced souls. The life she wins for us is not a mere fleshly life, though she obtains for men bodily favors also, but

[215] Encyclical *Mystici Corporis Christi.*
[216] *Ibid.*
[217] Leo XIII, Encyclical *Octobri mense adventante,* Sept. 22, 1891.

a share in the fulness of her Son's grace, life in and through Christ, our grace-life, our divine life. Such grace Mary offers her dear ones to help them form, renew and increase daily their life of holiness.

Truly Mary guides our every step along the path to Heaven. We become her children when through Baptism we join her Son's Mystical Body; and all our days she seeks to form in us the life of Christ. From birth till death each grace we receive bears Mary's touch because by God's will all grace comes to men through her prayers. Moreover, our souls can neither stay holy nor reach Heaven unless we live as devoted children of Our Lady. Her messages and appearances in the last century —to St. Catherine Labouré at Paris, to St. Bernadette at Lourdes, to the children at Fatima—all show our Mother's interest in the eternal welfare of her family. "May she, then, most holy Mother of all Christ's members . . . never cease to beg from Him that a continuous copious flow of graces may pass from its glorious Head into all the members of the Mystical Body." [218]

[218] Encyclical *Mystici Corporis Christi.*

CHAPTER FIFTEEN: *A Christ-Life*

I

THIS is God's plan for our salvation. Having pity on His people sunk in sin and lost to Heaven, God the Father asked His Son to save mankind; God the Son agreed. So at the appointed time the Son took our flesh; and in that flesh the God-man lived a life of lowly service and bore a cruel Passion and Crucifixion. By such suffering He won for men all the graces of holiness and salvation they would ever need. Moreover, precisely because He is the God-man, our Savior has the right to dispense these very graces.

Jesus is both God and man, the Child both of Heaven and of earth. As the Son of God He enjoys the identical divine life which His Father possesses. As man He has a human life like our own; furthermore, so perfectly are man and God united in Him that His human nature possesses a divine life also, the life of God the Son. "For in him dwelleth all the fulness of the Godhead corporeally." [219] Ordinarily it belongs to God alone to possess life truly divine. Hence when man receives this life, it comes as a tremendous gift, as a supernatural life. Thus does the human nature of Jesus enjoy the divine life of God as a supernatural life.

However, though God's own life and holiness were His, our Savior received into His soul sanctifying grace also. For that grace was to be the source and cause of His meritorious deeds, as it is for us. Again the grace of holiness beautified Our Lord's soul as it does ours—indeed, far more than it beautifies our souls. Yet, while Jesus needed sanctifying grace in order thereby to make His deeds meritorious, it was largely for man's sake that He accepted this grace. In the Creed recited at Mass the priest says that Our Lord "for us men and for our salvation descended from Heaven and became incarnate." If the Son of God became man for our sake, certainly He was thinking largely of us when He added sanctifying grace to His human nature. How so?

God wanted to share with men His own life and holiness. Of ourselves we could not receive the genuinely divine life and holiness, as Our Lord's human nature received it. Once only did man possess God's own living holiness—when the Son of God took our flesh. How then would God share with us His life and holiness? In that way in which the wise God could fit it into man's weak created nature, in that way in which man's weak created nature could receive it—namely, through a special gift made for the purpose, through a favor rooted in eternal love, through a grace that would mirror in us God's own

[219] Col. 2:9.

life and holiness, that would make us holy in our very
being, that would give us a divine vitality and that would
help us to earn Heaven. That gift, by which God lets us
partake of His holy life, we call sanctifying grace. Even
in our Savior this grace is a share of the divine life and
holiness which He enjoys as man; it is a living image, a
created likeness, a limited share of God's holiness. Sanctifying grace made Adam holy to a heavenly degree; it
gives us what we call the divine life. Such power has
God planted in sanctifying grace that, as long as it enlivens our souls, we are truly holy in His sight and live
a life closest to His own. Thus, when God bestows this
gift on men, He really shares with them His own life
and holiness.

We said that Our Lord received sanctifying grace into
His soul largely for our sake, for our holiness and salvation. That should not surprise us because Jesus offered
His every deed and His very life for us. See what He has
done for men in the order of grace! He took our flesh
in order that He might restore sanctifying grace to us.
He won all graces for all men. He left us His Church,
the home of saints, to be our home. He gave us the
sacraments and the Mass to make us holy. He taught us
to pray so that we might win grace. He guides the
Church all days till the end of time, "always living to
make intercession for us." [220] He accepted sanctifying
grace into His soul eternally because, if He would be for
all centuries the source and the lord and the model of
such grace, it was fitting that He Himself possess this
very grace.

[220] Heb. 7:25.

The Life That Is Grace

Jesus is the model of our grace-life: by possessing sanctifying grace while on earth He showed us how a soul in the state of grace should live. Jesus is the lord of our grace-life. He is the king of all. His "kingdom is not of this world." [221] His is a spiritual kingdom, the kingdom of Heaven, which calls all men to grace and virtue—"a kingdom of truth and life, a kingdom of holiness and grace." [222] Jesus is the source of our grace-life. Every grace we receive is granted because by His Passion Our Lord won all grace for mankind. From the moment of Adam's sin till the end of the world, He has offered and will offer to men all the grace they need. For example, Our Lady was given the grace of her Immaculate Conception because of her Son's future sufferings. Again, notice the number of prayers in which the Church begs God the Father for grace "through Jesus Christ Our Lord." But not only *through* Jesus do we obtain grace; He Himself dispenses it to us. He surely merited grace for men; yet even before He suffered, He had the right to distribute grace to mankind precisely because He was the God-man. So in the New Testament He personally dispenses all graces. He is the treasurer of divine riches. Thus at Baptism He gives men their first gift of sanctifying grace. For the rest of our days we gain further sanctifying grace as Christ wishes or as we earn it; and each added grace is measured in amount according to the sacraments we receive, our devotion and love in receiving them, our virtuous deeds and our degree of holiness at the time. Daily our Savior dispenses

[221] John 18:36.
[222] Preface, Mass of Christ the King.

135

to us added measures of grace and so shows Himself to us as the center and source of our grace-life. Was it not for man's heavenly welfare that Jesus took within His soul the grace called sanctifying?

Of course Our Lord enjoys this grace in full measure. Indeed, He holds the fulness of grace as His own personal right forever. "And the Word was made flesh and dwelt amongst us . . . full of grace and truth." [223] "And of his fulness we have all received, and grace for grace." [224] How do we receive of Christ's fulness? Not as if He contained within Himself every single grace that the human race has received or will receive; not as if His soul actually housed the individual graces offered to men. Moreover, even when Our Lord dispenses graces to us, His fulness of grace never lessens. But our Savior lets us partake of His fulness by giving each of us a personal share of sanctifying grace which resides in our soul and which makes us holy. What we thus receive is our own personal grace, separate from Christ's, like His in kind though differing in amount. Our Savior possesses the fullest measure of sanctifying grace, a degree of holiness which all men together can never reach; we receive a limited amount of grace which, however, we can enlarge with every virtuous deed we do. "All power is given to me in Heaven and in earth," [225] said Our Lord. With that power Jesus, as the moment comes, produces in men's souls each baptismal grace which starts the divine life, each added grace which builds up the divine

[223] John 1:14.
[224] John 1:16.
[225] Matt. 28:18.

life, and lastly the final height of grace in which God's children go to their judgment. Thus, because He is for us the source and lord and model of a grace so like His own, we have a Christlike holiness and can call our grace-life a Christ-life.

II

Jesus is "the life." [226] "In him was life." [227] In their fulness He has divine life, human life and the grace-life. He holds power over the life of grace: "For as the Father . . . giveth life: so the Son also giveth life to whom he will." [228] In fact, only through Christ can men obtain the grace-life. "I am . . . the Life. No man cometh to the Father but by me." [229] We say the saints and Our Lady win graces for us. Really this happens because Jesus, hearing their prayers to Himself, deigns to answer them favorably; for through Him alone do we gain our divine life.

Sanctifying grace is a living holiness on the divine level, man's greatest share here of God's life. Using His power to give "life to whom He will," Our Lord communicates the life of grace to us steadily. "For . . . Christ Jesus Himself, as the head into the members and the vine into the branches, continually infuses strength into those justified . . . without which they could not in any manner be pleasing and meritorious before God." [230]

[226] John 11:25.
[227] John 1:4.
[228] John 5:21.
[229] John 14:6.
[230] Council of Trent, *Decree on Justification*, Chap. 16.

And what a rich life our Savior sends us! The grace-life means we are holy in our inmost selves; the divine life is most intimately united with our soul. Moreover, those who live the grace-life have a right to sufficient help from God and to the reward they win. Hence Our Lord strengthens our divine life with power from on high. "In us the nerves reach from the head to all parts of the body and give them the power to feel and move; in like manner our Savior communicates power to His Church." [231] For instance, He gives us virtues and actual graces whence we draw vital strength to do deeds after His example and so live up to the high dignity of our grace-life. In addition, because by such deeds we merit added grace, Jesus builds up our divine life so that it thrives more vigorously. Again, the God-man Himself possesses the Holy Spirit: "The Spirit of the Lord is upon me." [232] Lovingly, as He did with the Apostles, He shares with us His own divine Spirit: "Now if any man have not the Spirit of Christ, he is none of his." [233] Behold the one Spirit in each soul living the godly life—and that, the Spirit of Jesus! Does not Christ labor to fulfill Himself in us, His brothers? The Savior's grace-life included the life itself—sanctifying grace, the Spirit of life, and the strength proper to that life—virtues. He used the further power of actual grace; He merited by His works. All these gifts formed Christ's grace-life and He has fitted them into our grace-life. Is He not forming in us a Christ-life much like His own?

[231] Encyclical *Mystici Corporis Christi.*
[232] Luke 4:18.
[233] Rom. 8:9.

Surely our divine life depends very greatly on Jesus. At Baptism, when we were born of His Father, He gave us our start in the life of grace. We became, like Christ, living sons of God. From then on He constantly tended our soul-life so that it would grow more like His own. In living the grace-life God's child does many virtuous acts each day; and after each deed our Savior further enlivens our heavenly life. Thus He communicates divine life to us frequently, steadily, all our days. St. Paul calls Christ a "quickening spirit" [234] for the resurrection of the body; just as truly is He a vivifying spirit for our soul-life. Through His graces He helps each person in every spiritual advance. He guides all supernatural life to greater heights of holiness; through His gifts He leads each man along his own personal path of holiness—in marriage or at the altar or in a lumber-yard, as a soldier or an office-worker or a teacher. If men take on a mature vitality in their divine life, it is due largely to the gifts of life which Jesus granted them so lovingly and lavishly. With St. Paul we can say "Christ is your life." [235]

This the Master Himself taught us in the parable of the vine and the branches.[236] He is the Vine, the Vine-stock in which the branches live. The latter are holy souls, each called to be a branch of the true Vine. The fruit mentioned in the parable is that which God the Father as the heavenly Husbandman and Christ as the Vine desire from men, that is, virtuous deeds worthy of life eternal. The influence of the vine on the branches

[234] I Cor. 15:45.
[235] Col. 3:4.
[236] John 15:1ff.

parallels Our Lord's influence on us. For He is "the true Vine": as the vine in the branches, He produces life-giving results in us. Indeed, if the branches are to bear fruit, the vine's influence on them is absolutely necessary; so too Christ's influence on us, if we would bear spiritual fruit. To fulfill this happy purpose, the vine and its branches possess an identical being and life; our Savior and holy souls enjoy a similar grace-life and the identical Spirit of life. Moreover, the branches must be so intimately joined to the vine that together they form but one living plant; Christ and His brethren must likewise be intimately united in their grace-life and form the one living Body. The severed branch is deprived of the vine's life-giving strength and so bears no fruit. In like manner, a soul which neglects the vital impulses of grace and sins mortally renders itself unworthy to receive the gifts of our divine life, thereby cuts itself off from the life-giving Christ and the Holy Spirit of life, and makes itself a dying branch of the true Vine. Only the branch which is vitally united to the vine bears fruit; so too, when we are vitally united to Jesus by faith and charity, can we do virtuous deeds. In fact, as the fruit shows the branch's oneness with the vine, so heavenly deeds prove a holy person's bond with our Savior.

Here in the parable the Master goes a step further. Not only ought the branch be joined to the vine but the vine should be united to the branches. "Abide in me and I in you." The branch does not live in the vine unless the vine lives in the branch; the branch will not thrive on the vine unless the vine inserts its life into the branch. "He that abideth in me and I in him, the same beareth much fruit: for without me you can do nothing." Hence there must be a mutual union between Christ and His brethren in the Father's household. Certainly we should be joined with Our Lord in order to live like Him; at the same time Christ, choosing to need us as members of His Church and co-workers in His mission of salvation, lavishly extends and inserts His grace-life into us. God has made vine and branch into one plant; and, thus united, they live and work for each other so that the branch by bearing fruit may honor the vine. God also has joined the true Vine and His branches into a living unity. Therein Christ and we must toil and live for each other so that we, the branches, may by our holy deeds glorify Christ, the Vine. The crowning glory of the vine, for which it spends itself, is the ripe fruit its branches yield.

What have we learned so far from the parable? We absolutely need Christ's influence on our souls. His help does not make easy for us deeds which human strength alone might do; rather, it enables us to work super-human wonders which manly power can neither start nor finish. Thus to live, act and grow in Christlike holiness, we branches vitally need the Vine's influence. For while the vine depends on the branches somewhat, the branch depends on the vine all the way from its birth through its growth and maturity. Hence vine and branch must be intimately joined in one life; there must be a mutual living union between vine and branch. The branch is inserted into the vine; the vine, prolonging its own life, inserts itself into the branch. So Christ and His own are vitally and mutually united in one living Body.

The branch is the vine extending its own living self;
holy souls are Christ extending His own grace-life by
giving us a like grace-life. Are we not Christ? Has He
not gifted us with a Christ-life?

Christ and we, living in each other, are ready to fulfill our vocation. The husbandman expects to gather
from the branches a rich harvest; God the Father calls
us, branches of the true Vine, to offer Him fruits of
Christ-like devotion, penance, courage and love. The
power to carry out its vocation the branch draws from
the vine: we receive our heavenly strength from Jesus.
The influence the vine exerts on the branch is interior.
External forces also—for example, sun and air—help the
vine to grow and the branches to yield grapes, but the
vine influences the very inmost being and life and work
of its branches. So too does Our Lord influence His
members most intimately. Other forces move us to virtue
from without—reading, advice, sermons, example; and
even our Savior stirs us in this way to follow Him. However, as the Vine, Christ does not influence His branches
from without; He touches our inmost being—our soul,
our mind and will—from within. Not by a merely external picturing of Christ are we live members of the
Vine but by the inward life of grace thriving within us.
The influence of the vine on the branches is life-giving.
The vine by nourishing the branch sustains it in life; the
living sap of the vine carries health, vigor and growth to
the tip of each branch. Christ affects men by giving them
life—indeed, a divine life. This life the Vine quickens
through the grace that enlivens. Branches on the vine
may be tiny or large; the member of Christ may be a

newborn child of God or a person alive with mature holiness. Yet, however far His branches extend, the influence of Christ reaches to them and floods them with the more abundant life. Using the strength supplied by the vine, the branch grows larger, more powerful and more fruitful. Branches must take the help offered them by a vine; men, however, are free to reject or accept Christ's helping graces. But when we will to use His graces of holiness and courage and devotion and perseverance, we become larger and more vigorous and more fruitful branches of our Savior. We are more vitally joined to the Vine, more intimately one with Him, more firmly fixed in Him, more fully a branch of His, more abidingly in Him and He in us, more graced with His life, more fruitful in His work. "Christ is your life." [237] Our divine life is a Christ-life.

III

As branches depend on the vine for their life, so we depend on Christ, the Vine, for our life as His branches. From Him to Catholics in the state of grace a living bond of holiness extends, so that our grace-life becomes a Christ-life. God calls men to attain and preserve this life through virtuous deeds; and if we fail thus to guard our Christ-life, we must suffer unending death in Hell. "If anyone abide not in me, he shall be cast forth as a branch and shall wither and they shall gather him up and cast him into the fire and he burneth." [238] See the first benefit of our Christ-life: it saves us from the worst calamity

[237] Col. 3:4.
[238] John 15:6.

that strikes men—the eternal failure of the damned soul; it helps us to do deeds worthy of Heaven and it fits us to live forever with Jesus in our Father's house.

Other benefits of our grace-life the Savior shows us in His parable of the vine and the branches.[239] If by rejecting serious temptations we remain living and growing branches of the true Vine, God will hear our prayers. These, unlike the sinner's prayer, gain a worth and power which draw God to answer them. "If you abide in me . . . you shall ask whatever you will and it shall be done unto you." [240] The husbandman takes honor from the fruit on his vines; by the fruits of generosity and sacrifice and charity and devotion we glorify our Father and Christ's Father. "In this is my Father glorified, that you bring forth very much fruit." [241] As long as we obey the Commandments, we shall grow in our Christ-life and in our Savior's love for us. We shall abide in His love and He in ours; He will pour His grace of love into His branches while we offer Him our love. "I also have loved you. Abide in my love. If you keep my commandments, you shall abide in my love." [242] Our Lord makes the keeping of His Commandments the rule for abiding in the Christ-life and in His love; for instance, when He met a man who had observed the Commandments from his youth, "Jesus, looking on him, loved him." [243] Through our Christ-life, furthermore, we partake to the full of Christ's joy. "These things I have

[239] John 15:7–11.
[240] John 15:7.
[241] John 15:8.
[242] John 15:9–10.
[243] Mark 10:21.

spoken to you that my joy may be in you and your joy may be filled." [244] So do we depend on Christ. Without His gifts of love and life, naught worthy of Heaven can be started. With our Christ-life we pray worthily and win blessings, we live virtuously and honor our Father, we observe God's law and share our Savior's love and joy.

We said that souls in grace are joined to Christ by a living bond. How can one person have a real living union with another? We shall try through pictures to give some idea of our intimate oneness with Christ.

A ship, battered by the seas, broadcasts a plea for help. The answering vessel shoots a rope across the water to the disabled ship. That rope links the two ships and carries the crew of the wounded vessel to safety. The rope acts as a life-line every inch of the way; it gives life to the endangered seamen as it transports them over the water. The bond of grace links souls to Jesus in a living unity; it is a life-line because it saves us from Hell and gives us eternal life all our days.

In every tree there exists a life-line of continuous living cells from the deepest root-end to the highest leaf. This ensures life and growth and beauty and fruitfulness in the tree's branches. The grace which links us to our Head, Christ, is a real life-line, binding us members to one another in Jesus and giving us a divine beauty of soul.

In a transfusion, rich healthy blood enters the veins of a sick person. That blood acts as a life-line, bringing needed strength to weak bodies. The life-line of grace

[244] John 15:11.

comes from the strong Christ to men fighting the enemies of holiness and gives us the vital power and courage to win Heaven.

A baby, both before and at birth, is joined to its mother by a real tie of flesh. That cord is truly a life-line, for it links mother and child in such a living oneness that the mother lives in the child and the latter in the mother. Through the tie of flesh, moreover, the mother nourishes her little one and so gives life and increase to her infant. No wonder parents call children their own flesh and blood! The link between mother and babe is a cord of flesh, the cord of Adam; hence the newborn child is another Adam and a son of man.

The babe at Baptism is born a son of God and so begins its divine life. Moreover, the baptismal grace—a very real, spiritual, supernatural gift within the soul—unites the child to Our Lord. That grace acts as the cord of Christ. It links the new child of God to our Savior in a living bond; it is Christ's gift of life to us; because of it Jesus imparts to us the other gifts of the divine life—for instance, the Eucharist, wherein Our Lord nourishes and increases our life as His brothers. So the newly baptized becomes another Christ, living the Christ-life.

The cord of flesh which united mother and infant is cut, so that the babe must nourish itself and live its own separate life, no longer to live in its mother. Christ will never cut off from Himself the holy Catholic but, as we act virtuously, He will continue to pour into us ever larger shares of His grace-life. Hence we shall be united to Him more intimately, more vitally and more sacredly. He will live in us—and we in Him—more abundantly.

Thus our divine life is our personal life of holiness and at the same time a Christ-life. So close and mutual a bond exists between our Savior and each graced person! Truly sanctifying grace is our life-line, linking Christ and ourselves in a vital intimacy and a living union.

IV

A close likeness usually marks the members of a family. They enjoy a similar flesh and blood; often they have the same shape of the head or color of the eyes, the same size and figure. Sometimes their actions are alike: they walk or talk in a common way; they may even have like virtues : courtesy and generosity.

Into His family God, our Maker and Father, calls all men. He expects us as members of the divine family to be like Him in every way we can—"perfect as also your heavenly Father is perfect." [245] Accordingly God started man in life by making him to His own image and likeness.[246] He gave us a power to think and to choose, which lifts man above the animals of the field and mirrors His own mind and will. Besides, God poured into man's soul the grace of holiness that we might enjoy a divinely holy life. So were we fitted to guard and enlarge the image of God within us. That image we can deface by sin, but our vocation summons us to grow daily more like God.

Moreover, God not only equipped us to live like Himself, He showed us how to imitate Him by giving us for a model His own Son in the flesh, Jesus Christ, who

[245] Matt. 5:48.
[246] Gen. 1:26–27.

would live our human life in order to teach men by word and example how to live the divine life. "The reason why the only-begotten Son of the eternal Father wished to be a Son of man was that we might be made conformed to the image of the Son of God and be renewed according to the image of Him who created us." [247] Thus by following our Savior we fulfill our vocation to imitate the heavenly Father.

For Christ is the perfect Image of His Father and ours. In His Godhead Jesus possesses the identical life, love and holiness which the Father has; and, through its fulness of sanctifying grace, His is the human nature most perfectly like God. Jesus is our finest model. Ever intimate with His divine Father, He enjoys also the close companionship of His Spirit, the Holy Ghost. The virtues He practiced in their perfection. Well could God the Father say of our Savior at His Baptism [248] and at His Transfiguration: "This is my beloved Son in whom I am well pleased." [249] What holiness men and even saints have in part, He has in the fullest. Every virtue we practice, Christ finely models for us. Such perfect example are we called and privileged to imitate! "For whom he foreknew, he also predestinated to be made conformable to the image of His Son." [250]

How shall we sons of God imitate the first-born Son of God? "But put ye on the Lord Jesus Christ." [251] We must put on Christ in our divine life. That life is mainly

[247] Encyclical *Mystici Corporis Christi.*
[248] Matt. 3:17.
[249] Matt. 17:5.
[250] Rom. 8:29.
[251] Rom. 13:14.

interior; we must, then, strive to be interiorly like our Savior—to live the inward life of holiness, to be a truly holy Christian and Catholic, to walk the Christlike way of holiness and virtue. Our Lord does not want us to imitate Him only outwardly, to the eyes of men. "And Christ died for all: that they also who live, may not now live to themselves but unto him who died for them." [252]

The life in which we live "unto Him" and imitate Him interiorly begins at Baptism. Therein Jesus beholds the inward powers we have as man and pours into them a share of His divine life and strength. This wonder He works by enlivening our soul with the baptismal grace of sanctity, by adding to our mind the virtue of faith and by instilling into our will the virtues of hope and charity. Through these gifts Christ makes our interior life of holiness the image of His own, as far as it can be here. We have put on Christ interiorly, "for as many of you as have been baptized in Christ, have put on Christ." [253]

Henceforth our vocation calls us to put on Christ more and more by using His gifts. Without that all else is trifling, because the child of God who does not use grace and the virtues is in danger of losing his eternal life. "For we are made partakers of Christ: yet so, if we hold the beginning of his substance firm unto the end." [254] Only the man who lives the divine life of grace steadily continues to be a true likeness of the Man who is God, Christ.

Thus to imitate Jesus we must practice the virtues He

[252] II Cor. 5:15.
[253] Gal. 3:27.
[254] Heb. 3:14.

gave us and so increase our divine life and strength. "For let this mind be in you which was also in Christ Jesus." [255] We must put on our Savior's "mind." St. Paul does not mean merely the power to think but the mentality, attitudes, interests and desires of Our Lord. These we put on through the virtues received in Baptism. By faith, for instance, we accept as from our Savior's lips the teachings He left to His Church and we believe them on His word. We ponder these truths in prayer, begging the Holy Spirit to enlighten us on their meaning and use. Then with the help of grace we live our faith. As apostles, we spread the truths Christ taught us, we defend them, we act according to them. We make faith inspire, as it ought, each holy deed we do. Faith colors our life so that our works are Catholic works. Thus we live up to our faith and deserve to be called "the faithful." Our Christlike deeds bear witness that we are living by the teachings of the Master. "I live in the faith of the Son of God." [256]

Besides faith, Jesus enriches our divine life with the virtue of hope which He instills into our will. For to hope faith leads us surely. "Now faith is the substance of things to be hoped for." [257] Faith gives us a firm persuasion that through Christ our hopes will be fulfilled—our hope for God's help here and for Heaven hereafter. We who are baptized in Christ must place all our trust in Him and in the triune God. Nor will our acts of hope be weak or fearful; rather, they will be firm and strong.

[255] Phil. 2:5.
[256] Gal. 2:20.
[257] Heb. 11:1.

For our hope rests on "God who lieth not" [258] but is true to His promises. Moreover, God the Father sent His Son Jesus to die for men and so to strengthen our hope [259] for holiness and salvation. Then too He gives us the Holy Spirit, who, by living within and sanctifying our soul, is God's loving guarantee of our hopes. "And hope confoundeth not: because the charity of God is poured forth in our hearts by the Holy Ghost who is given to us." [260] Indeed, the Blessed Trinity, dwelling within us Itself, goes surety that our hope in the divine promises will be honored.

Thus armed with a mighty confidence, we use our virtue of hope. We daily expect from God the graces which will enable us to abide and grow in our divine life. By increasing our holiness our hope becomes stronger and we grow more worthy to receive eternal blessedness. The hope of gaining Heaven enters all our virtuous deeds. That hope inspires us to imitate our Savior in our every action; it spurs us on to avoid mortal sin; it sustains us while we strive for greater holiness; it comforts us in trial and in sorrow; it supports the dying child of God; and it carries us into life eternal.

The water of Baptism brings into our divine life yet a third virtue by which we can put on Christ—charity. Like hope, this virtue is closely knit to faith. For the man living by faith truly loves God; and the Catholic, inspired by charity, gladly believes God. We other Christs have "faith in your hearts . . . being rooted and

[258] Titus 1:2.
[259] Rom. 5:5–11.
[260] Rom. 5:5.

founded in charity." [261] Through charity we gain the strength to love God for Himself and men for God. That love enables us to forget self and to labor entirely for God and neighbor.

In the divine life charity and sanctifying grace go hand in hand. If we do not love God, we are cold to Him, we disobey His Commandments; and the keeping of those Commandments is the rule for lasting love between God and man. "He that hath my commandments and keepeth them, he it is that loveth me." [262] No wonder the graces of holiness and charity are always united! So where serious sin abides, love of God fails and without solid love holiness withers. Indeed, without charity nothing else avails in the divine life. "And if I should have prophecy and should know all mysteries and all knowledge and if I should have all faith so that I could remove mountains, and have not charity, I am nothing. And if I should distribute all my goods to feed the poor and if I should deliver my body to be burned, and have not charity, it profiteth me nothing." [263] Hence charity is our greatest and most necessary virtue. It averts serious faults in that selfishness which marks every sin; one who lives in charity will not sin mortally but will grow in sanctity. Moreover, charity in action leads us into all kinds of holy deeds. "Charity is patient, is kind . . . seeketh not her own . . . thinketh no evil . . . rejoiceth with the truth, beareth all things, believeth all things, hopeth all things, endureth all things." [264] Under God we

[261] Eph. 3:17.
[262] John 14:21.
[263] I Cor. 13:2–3.
[264] I Cor. 13:4–7.

Catholics are brothers and sisters of Christ and of each other; charity preserves and fulfills that divine brotherliness. "Loving one another with the charity of brotherhood." [265] Yet we of God's family are called to love and labor for all men as Jesus did, even for those who hate us. "Love your enemies . . . that you may be the children of your Father who is in Heaven." [266] Here too charity helps us to love our persecutors and to act as men born of God. That we may bestow such love on God and men as befits our divine childhood, the Father has given us not alone the virtue of charity but also the Holy Ghost, the Spirit of love. "And because you are sons, God hath sent the Spirit of his Son into your hearts, crying Abba: Father." [267] Through this twofold gift we can love our heavenly Father, calling out to Him with a cry of affection; and in our common Father we can love all men. Behold the work of our grace-life: to love God and man with a holy and divine charity.

With charity, then, we shall love with a divine love. That virtue will make all our deeds loving deeds; without it there will be no thought or deed worthy of Heaven; our love of God and man will enter as a motive into all our virtuous actions (it must, so closely knit is charity to holiness); it will stir us to toil for God and neighbor, even at the cost of humbling self; every work we do in our divine life will be the affectionate voice of our charity for God and men.

Such a life of charity St. Paul calls the "more excellent

[265] Rom. 12:10.
[266] Matt. 5:44-45.
[267] Gal. 4:6.

way." [268] In walking that way of life our Savior helps us constantly. Through His gift of Holy Communion, when we receive Him worthily and thankfully, He implants in our hearts an ever stronger love of God and man, with which we can love all He loves. And what wonders of charity does He not work in us so that our loves and desires may be those of His Sacred Heart! Thus the Eucharistic Jesus fosters in His younger brothers and sisters the greatest of virtues, the heart of holiness and "the culmination of the law." [269]

Furthermore, Our Lord gives us as our guest the Holy Ghost, His own Spirit of love. Through that divine Breath of charity God the Father and God the Son love each other forever; in that same divine Spirit of charity we shall love our heavenly Father, our Brother Christ, the Holy Ghost Himself and our fellow men. Yet our acts of charity bring into our soul not only the Holy Spirit but the Father and the Son also. "If any one love me . . . my Father will love him and we will come to him and will make our abode with him." [270] Within us the three divine Persons dwell as in Heaven—loving each other, loving the soul which houses them and loving all holy souls. In turn we, who welcome God under our roof, will love our Guests, the indwelling Trinity, and with them all souls in grace. To such mutual union and intimacy with God and man does holy charity lead us! Lastly, this virtue deepens our likeness to Christ and to God. By charity we imitate our Savior. "As I have loved

[268] I Cor. 12:31.
[269] Rom. 13:10.
[270] John 14:23.

you, that you also love one another." [271] Again, our
works of charity make us like God, who "is charity" [272]
entirely and always. Thus by the practice of charity we
fill out ever more the image of Christ and of God in us;
we grow ever more like unto Christ and God.

We have seen how to use faith, hope and charity in
our grace-life. Our Savior picks these three virtues for us
as those mainly helpful in the divine life. They must influence all our holy deeds so that every act bespeaks our
Catholic faith, our hope of Heaven, our love for God
and man. Moreover, these virtues are implanted in us so
that by possessing them we may put on Christ interiorly
and by practicing them we may according to our vocation grow ever more like Him. Jesus wants us to live by
faith, hope and charity and thus to put on His mind, His
will and His heart as by sanctifying grace we take on the
likeness of His soul. The holy Catholic today resembles
the early Christian in the days of the Apostles: "The
multitude of believers had but one heart and one
soul." [273] The one heart, one soul, one mind and one will
we have through grace and the virtues are Christ's. The
Church on earth spends herself in securing this happy
result. "My little children, of whom I am in labor again
until Christ be formed in you." [274] With St. Paul, Christ's
Church calls us her children. Like a mother, she labors
to beget us as other Christs. In her anxiety for us and in
her work for our salvation she suffers the pains of child-

[271] John 13:34.
[272] I John 4:8.
[273] Acts 4:32.
[274] Gal. 4:19.

birth in order that we may be formed anew in Christ and may put on Christ more firmly and more completely all the days of our life.

Lastly, faith, hope and charity are precisely the virtues concerned with God; their use helps us to be attentive and united to God, as was Christ in His stay on earth. By faith, hope and charity we of the divine family believe, trust and love our Father in Heaven. What would our divine life—or any life—be if we could not believe, trust and love God? Yes, these virtues play a large part in our grace-life. They are the mark, the family likeness of God's children. They center our thoughts and desires on God, three in one. They enable us to put on Christ interiorly and so to expand our likeness to God.

CHAPTER SIXTEEN: *The Life of the Mystical Body*

I

THE Church Our Lord founded we call the Roman Catholic Church. That Church, ever alive with grace and virtue, is the Mystical Body of Christ. At this moment the members of the Catholic Church are Jesus, glorious in Heaven, and the faithful now on earth. The first member is the real actual Christ, enjoying the fulness of grace and life; we who have been truly baptized, maintain the Catholic faith and give obedience to the Catholic Church, are her other members. The Mystical Body, then, is made up of the Savior and the Catholic faithful, even those in serious sin. Neither alone suffices; we certainly need Christ and He deigns to need us in forming His Mystical Body.

In this Body a mystic bond unites Jesus and ourselves. We are not merely a group working for a common purpose, like a club or a team. Husband and wife are "two in one flesh," [275] but our bond with Jesus is far above the

[275] Gen. 2:24.

world of flesh. Christ and we are brothers and sisters in God's family; yet the tie that binds us together in the Mystical Body surpasses the ties of blood and love which unite a human family. Our bond with Jesus is the Holy Spirit, Christ's own Spirit of holiness dwelling in Him and in sanctified souls.

In Catholic sinners the Holy Spirit has already dwelt and He has intimately helped them to live the divine life. Moreover, even when Catholics by mortal sin lose that Spirit, a remnant of the grace-life survives within them. They still enjoy the virtues of faith and hope; the baptismal character still marks them as persons who have taken on the likeness of Christ and are dedicated to His service; they still continue loyal to the Church; with God's grace they can be restored to that holiness which is the healthy life of the Mystical Body. This remnant of divine life, though it leaves sinners weak members of Christ, enables them to remain in the Mystical Body. A person can be racked with disease, but while he lives, he still has hope and is counted among the living; the sinful Catholic is a prostrate member of his Church but he still has faith and hope and he still continues to be a part of that Body. "For not every sin, however grave and enormous it be, is such as to sever a man automatically from the Body of the Church, as does schism or heresy or apostasy. Men may lose charity and divine grace through sin and so become incapable of supernatural merit, and yet not be deprived of all life if they hold on to faith and Christian hope, and illumined from above they are spurred on by the strong promptings of the Holy Spirit to salutary fear and by God are moved to prayer and penance for their sins." [276]

Since the Holy Spirit links Christ and ourselves, our mystic union is sacred and supernatural. Moreover, because our holiness is a divine life, the Mystical Body knits Christ and us in a living, vital bond. In order to enter this Body we must be born of God and take on the grace-life; then, joined to Christ, who has the grace-life in its completeness, we form with Him His Body. Hence the Mystical Body is a living body as truly alive as the flowering plant.

The mystic union is a very real bond between Christ and each Catholic, between Christ and all Catholics, and through Christ between Catholics themselves. We are all bound together in a living unity. Within that unity Christ, God and man, is the Head and we are the members. With us Jesus shares His grace-life and His Holy Spirit; He would bestow His gifts on all men if only they would accept Him.[277] Actually He shares with us even His own Self. For in the Eucharist He nourishes His members on the identical food, His divine Flesh and Blood. No wonder an identical divine life vitalizes the Mystical Body through all its parts! Besides, our Savior gives us Himself to be our Head in His Mystical Body. Indeed, as our virtuous acts deserve, He grants us a fuller grace-life, stronger virtues and a deeper intimacy with God. Moreover, He gives us rich graces of action according to our needs and His plans for us. Thus we other Christs can do and are called to do the work of

[276] Encyclical *Mystici Corporis Christi.*
[277] John 1:12.

Christ today by carrying out the spiritual tasks He shares with us. In His years on earth Jesus prayed, taught, healed, encouraged vocations, sought out souls, suffered, practiced virtue, forgave sins and ruled His flock. In Christ's Church today these tasks must still be done. Jesus will still do them through the members of His Body and through the actual graces He grants us. These members are many and varied, as befits their Head, who died for all men. There is the layman who by the grace of Christ preaches in the market place as did Jesus. A teen-age girl, inspired by grace, teaches religion to the public school children in a Christlike way. Grace from Our Lord aids the Catholic mother to train her little ones to godliness. The unmarried person through his use of grace gains a singular purity and zeal after the Heart of his divine Model. The riches of grace help the cloistered nun to pray in the Spirit of Christ. The suffering Catholic is stirred by grace to offer his agony and death for Christ's holy purposes. The grace of Holy Orders aids the priest to forgive sin with Christ. The graces of a foreign mission vocation give the missonary Christ's vocation of toiling far from home for the souls of men. Strong graces of courage assist the Holy Father to rule the Church as Christ's Vicar.

Do you see how throughout the world Catholics are linked to Christ? At every moment we are doing the work of Christ and we keep on doing it as other Christs —under His personal guidance, through His graces and because of our vital oneness with Him. Christ unites us all in a Christhood of charity, zeal, sacrifice, holiness and life. It is His Mystical Body deriving life and activity and direction and grace and growth and power from Christ Himself. It is Christ's Mystical Body—and no one else's.

Because we are mystically one with Him, Our Lord identifies us with Himself in a unique way. He treats us as Himself. He calls us by His own name. Each Christian in the Mystical Body is another Christ, and all together form the whole Christ. Any kindness or unkindness done to us He judges as done to Himself. "Amen, I say to you, as long as you did it to one of these my least brethren, you did it to me." [278] Our Savior loves us as Himself. In married life a husband should love his wife as his own body and his own self. "So also ought men to love their wives as their own bodies. He that loveth his wife, loveth himself." [279] Christ loves the members of Himself as His own Body which indeed they form, as His very Self which they truly are. "For no man ever hateth his own flesh but nourisheth and cherisheth it as also Christ does the Church. Because we are members of his body." [280] To our Redeemer "there is neither Jew nor Greek: there is neither bond nor free: there is neither male nor female"; [281] to Him we are, one and all, His own Self, Christ. "But Christ is all and in all." [282]

Our Lord said: "I am the light of the world." [283] "I am the way and the truth and the life." [284] Jesus in His life here preached that for men He was the path to Heaven:

[278] Matt. 25:40.
[279] Eph. 5:28.
[280] Eph. 5:29–30.
[281] Gal. 3:28.
[282] Col. 3:11.
[283] John 8:12.
[284] John 14:6.

"No man cometh to the Father but by me." [285] We who form Christ's Body and Church are still the way to Heaven open to all men. We of the Mystical Body have the truth Christ taught, for "we have the mind of Christ"; [286] by word and deed we still speak the Truth which is Christ. Each member of Christ is a light to men. "You are the light of the world." [287] "So let your light shine before men that they may see your good works and glorify your Father who is in Heaven." [288] Together with our Head we form the brightest and clearest Light "which enlighteneth every man that cometh into this world." [289] Christ is the Life; we Catholics live the Christ-life of grace. On earth Jesus was a living Light who illumined all He met; teaching that men must follow Him if they would gain Heaven, He showed Himself the living Way to the Father; revealing Himself as God and man, He presented Himself as the living Truth to be believed. Our Savior was the living Light on the living Way to living Truth. Today the Mystical Christ is yet the Way to the Truth, is yet the Light and the Life of the world.

Jesus is the Son of the Father and heir to His Father's kingdom; we are children of the Father and heirs to our Father's kingdom—in fact, "joint heirs with Christ." [290] In the Holy Sacrifice that is offered every day throughout the world, the Mystical Christ constantly offers the

[285] John 14:6.
[286] I Cor. 2:16.
[287] Matt. 5:14.
[288] Matt. 5:16.
[289] John 1:9.
[290] Rom. 8:17.

Lamb of Calvary as a Victim to His Father. Because that Sacrifice is the public worship of the Church, we who, though not present in body at Mass, are yet members of the Mystical Body, also offer with Christ the Victim of Calvary to our Father. Our prayer becomes the prayer of our Head, Christ, who presents it to God the Father. Our Lord's human deeds earned a divine reward—they honored the Father and so made up for the insult of man's sin; and they enabled Christ, the Son of Man, to sit at the Father's right hand in Heaven. Our deeds in Christ receive a divine reward also: the joyous vision of God forever and the eternal companionship of the Blessed Trinity.

We in the Mystical Body form one Christ, with each member a part of Him. "For you are all one in Christ Jesus." [291] This oneness between Christ and Catholics is a living bond, divinely unique. Indeed, our Savior compares it to the divine unity and identity between Himself and His Father: "That they may be one as we also are." [292] Jesus said: "The Father is in me and I in the Father." [293] In the Mystical Body Christ is in us and we are in Christ: "Abide in me and I in you." [294] Our Head lives by the Father while we live by Him. "As . . . I live by the Father, so he that eateth me . . . shall live by me." [295] God the Father loves His Son made man, and His Son loves us: "As the Father hath loved me, I also

[291] Gal. 3:28.
[292] John 17:11.
[293] John 10:38.
[294] John 15:4.
[295] John 6:58.

have loved you." [296] Once the Savior remarked to Philip: "He that seeth me, seeth the Father also." [297] In like manner those who with faith see us for all we mean to God, behold in us the living members of Christ—behold Christ Himself. "And this is the testimony that God hath given to us eternal life. And this life is in his Son. He that hath the Son, hath life." [298]

II

Each Catholic has been called in Baptism to an individual grace-life for whose growth he must answer to God. Yet men do not live only a personal life. World leaders ask us to take a global view of the human race; supernaturally we look at mankind from a viewpoint not only global but other-worldly, heavenly, divine. For, as a group, we who are baptized in Christ are the Catholic Church—which means the universal Church for all men of all times and places; together we individual Catholics form the Mystical Body of Christ.

Throughout this book we have treated the divine life of grace thriving in each sanctified soul. Now we would speak of our group life in the Catholic Church, of our family life as God's children in the Mystical Body; for what is true of our individual grace-life remains true in general of our united life as Christ's Body.

We said Our Lord came to give each of us life—not, however, a merely human or even angelic life but a life somehow divine. This life within our soul we call sanc-

[296] John 15:9.
[297] John 14:9.
[298] I John 5:11–12.

tifying grace. The Mystical Body is the group life Christ offers to all men. Its members are human beings, not angels; yet not as men only are we joined to Christ in living unity. Our Savior accepts us into His Body when through Baptism we have been born of God unto the divine life of grace, have taken up the faith Jesus taught and have become heirs of our Father's kingdom. Once Baptism grants us this life as God's children, Our Lord draws us into His Catholic Church, His mystical Self. Thus the Mystical Body enfolds within its Christ-life all who have individually received the divine life of grace and the Catholic faith. In His Body Christ shares with us His fulness of sanctifying grace.

For mankind the grace of holiness is a twice-given gift. First God gave it to all men through Adam, who lost it for his family. In time our Redeemer by His painful death restored it to the human race; He actually gives sanctifying grace to all who accept Him in His Church.[299] The Mystical Body could begin only after the Son of God became the God-man, for it is His Body; He completed it on Calvary. Hence, while the Mystical Body was given to mankind only once, the grace which vitalizes its members remains for the human race a twice-given gift. Indeed, how many more times Jesus has granted sanctifying grace to individuals who have sinned mortally, only God knows!

The grace of holiness dwells in our soul, which in turn penetrates the whole human body. The life of grace suffuses the entire Mystical Body in all its members. Only those who are truly baptized may enter Christ's Body,

[299] John 1:12.

though even the faithful Catholic in serious sin retains some divine life. Thus the Mystical Body in its Head and parts continues ever holy.

God has given each person a vocation to live the divine life here and so to enter into Heaven. That general call to possess sanctifying grace is included in a broader vocation to the Mystical Body. There can be Protestants who live in the state of grace but they are not members of Christ's Body, the Catholic Church, because they have not Catholic faith or obedience. Our vocation, then, is to receive the baptismal grace and also to join and to live till death in the Mystical Body. To such a life of holiness with Christ are all on earth destined.

The first gift of sanctifying grace to a soul makes one a new and different man. The sinner becomes holy; the child of men becomes God's child; while still on earth, the baptized person begins to live on a heavenly plane. Moreover, the millions of such men, who after Baptism practice Catholic faith and obedience, form a new order of being closest to God. Together with our Savior they make up the new man, the new Adam, the new Christ, the mystic Christ. This Mystical Body is a new level of life for which God finds a place next to Himself. By his holy deeds each Catholic in the state of grace advances to new virtue and takes on an ever new strength in his divine life. So too does the Catholic group grow in newness of virtue and sanctity. During Lent the faithful increase their penances; in May and October, devotion to the Blessed Mother reaches a new height; every day the Eucharistic Jesus is lovingly offered in Mass and received in Communion; Baptism leads new souls into the Church steadily; the priest's forgiveness of sin constantly renews the grace of life for his penitents; the family virtues daily sanctify the Catholic mother and father. Thus, as among Catholics over the world a new depth of suffering is accepted, a new height of holiness reached, a new breadth of charity exercised; as a more widespread devotion to Our Lady is practiced, a firmer faith professed before men, a new people converted to God, a more heroic courage shown in persecution; as a new religious order is founded, a greater place in family life given to Christ, a more Christlike priesthood formed, a warmer welcome extended to God's grace, and as each and every Catholic throughout the world carries out his part in these deeds, then the Mystical Body presents to God an ever fresh and pleasing newness. Indeed, our every act of virtue brings a constant newness of life to the Mystical Body. We have seen a gem so cut that at every turn it throws off a new brilliance of light and color. The Mystical Body is the living gem of God ever freshly reflecting Christ's holiness and life, ever newly alive with divine life, ever beautiful in its fulness of grace, ever lustrous in its variety of virtue, and every moment offering new glory to the Blessed Trinity. The Mystical Body, made up of new men in Christ, is itself the new Christ.

During its early years the baptized infant preserves its grace-life within its soul. At the age of reason the Catholic takes up the active life of holiness; from then till death he lives his religion both in his inward self and outwardly before his fellow men. Hence our divine life is both interior and exterior, though mainly interior. The Catholic is called to sanctify his soul and to help his neighbor to be holy, to bring himself and others to Heaven. In this double vocation we shall do many outward works of virtue, but our greater duty is to foster the inward life of grace which supports such works. The Mystical Body, like the individual Catholic, enjoys both an interior and exterior life of holiness, though again the interior life is more important. The mystic Christ is, first of all, the union of Himself and souls in the life of grace; and that grace is man's inward holiness. Hence the union of Catholics with Christ is mainly interior. Yet our group life in the Church also shows itself outwardly before the world. Men can behold the wealth of virtuous deeds done daily by Catholics; they know of our admirable leaders—priests, bishops and the Holy Father; they notice our universal work for the bodily and spiritual health of all peoples; they can read of the persecutions suffered by Catholics of all ages and ranks; they can see the growth of our Church here and in other lands. This means that the Mystical Body, the Catholic Church, is always clearly visible to mankind—a divine challenge and an invitation to every one. "Now since this social Body of Christ has been designed by its Founder to be visible, this co-operation of all its members must also be externally manifest through their profession of the same faith and their sharing of the same sacred rites, through participation in the same sacrifice and practical observance of the same laws. Above all, everyone must be able to see the Supreme Head." [300]

[300] Encyclical *Mystici Corporis Christi.*

Thus the Mystical Body is "a city seated on a mountain," [301] a candle "put upon a candlestick that it may shine to all." [302] Each Catholic is a flame drawing his neighbor's attention to his religion; all Catholics together form a world-wide flame showing every man where Jesus lives in His Church. This flame can be seen outwardly by mankind, but the oil supplying that flame remains ever our internal divine life of grace and virtue.

III

God wishes us to preserve and enlarge the divine life within us. Hence the individual grace-life is a life of growth in holiness and virtue. This growth begins after Baptism and progresses with each virtuous deed done in the state of grace. When, moreover, a person increases the number of holy works he does or deepens the devotion with which he does them, he advances in supernatural life and power more quickly. Our Catholic group life also is a life of growth. Daily the Church draws to herself newly baptized members. Again, every individual increase in grace means an increase of holiness in the Church; each act of virtue we do brings a growth in sanctifying grace to the Mystical Body. There are, furthermore, members of that Body who seek perfection avidly, who perform the works of Christ in the holiest fashion, who take on the virtues of Christ ever more fully; and these hasten the pace of growth in the mystic Christ. Thus the Mystical Body constantly advances in

[301] Matt. 5, 14.
[302] Matt. 5, 15.

the number of its members, in its divine life of holiness and in the depth of its virtues.

The sight of Catholics streaming to Sunday Mass in their parish churches makes us think of an army on the march, moving sturdily in review before its Leader. In truth the Mystical Body is an army on the march—strong, living, growing. Through the centuries it has been marching, straight from the hill of Calvary. At the head of His Mystical Body marches Christ, God and man. Then comes Peter, the first pope, with the Apostles and the disciples, searching the corners of the earth for new members of Christ's Body. Their converts follow them, presenting a united front [303] in faith and in prayer, in their possessions and at the Communion table. The martyrs in their agony confess Our Lord's doctrine while the Fathers of the Church teach and defend it. As time passes, the Mystical Body loses members by death and desertion but it is ever alive and growing, ever on the march. Behind Jesus and His pope move the hermits of the desert who have left all to live for God alone. Doctors of the Church, like Augustine, by their writings battle the heretics and strengthen the faithful to march in line with their priests. Missionaries like Patrick and Boniface move into strange lands, where they enlist new soldiers for Christ's army. Monks in their cells, preserving culture for the ages, and consecrated virgins, singing God's praise in prayer, take their place in the Mystical Body as confessors of the faith. The Crusaders, crying "God wills it," form in battle array to regain the Savior's homeland. Under their bishops the Catholic faithful—

[303] Acts 2:41–47.

the pure, the brave, the sick, the poor, the prayerful; the children, the kings and the queens, the workmen, the parents, the lawyers, the surgeons—all march through the years, ever remaining the heart of Christ's army and ever pleasing to the Father on high. St. Benedict, St. Francis of Assisi and St. Dominic lead the long line of religious men and women who wear the Cross of Christ for distinguished service. The Schoolmen move to their classes, where they teach the science of God and train their pupils for leadership in the Mystical Body. The theologians hasten to the great Councils of the Church. Foreign missionaries, like Xavier and Brebeuf and Claver, sail to far-off lands, always on the march for souls and always widening God's kingdom on earth. In step with them are the new races they have welcomed into the Church Militant.

Today the Mystical Body still marches, vital and sturdy. Today our Savior still leads His army, ever in the front rank. His is not an army on parade, marching down the main avenue of a city after final victory; Christ's army of conquerors rests happily in Heaven. The Mystical Body is an army in the field, in combat formation—marching over the whole world under orders from its Commander. Religious brothers and sisters move to their kneeling-bench, classroom, hospital, chapel, study-desk and to their place of toil in God's cause. The faithful—parents, nurses, scholars, painters, street-cleaners, school children, builders, teachers, laborers— all march with Our Lord, beautiful and joyous in the divine life which unites them as His soldiers. However outwardly they differ in color and citizenship and tongue and dress and wealth, they wear the same uniform—not one of braid and brass and stripe, but one of Christlike grace and virtue. Daily the newly baptized receive this uniform and join their comrades in the line of march. Today's confessors of Christ before men—the apostles of the Catholic press, workers of charity like St. Vincent de Paul, active spreaders of the faith in the Confraternity of Christian Doctrine, lay institutes and lay missionaries to foreign peoples—fulfill their vocation to labor in Our Lord's Church.

Truly the Mystical Body, as it moves through time, is rich in all kinds of virtue, like its Leader. Contemplatives, victim souls, penitents and frequent communicants give holy example to their comrades and win for them soldierly strength. The sick and the suffering, the martyrs jailed and beaten and slain for our faith live and die like heroes, in union with the Christ of Calvary. Over the wide world God's priests, from pope to youngest levite, are ever on the march to baptize, confirm, bury, console, teach, anoint, forgive, preach, witness Catholic marriage, offer Sacrifice and give Communion; for priests are in Holy Orders to bring Our Lord wherever He can help souls.

So the Mystical Body marches along through the years. Jesus is always its Head. By His grace He makes each member another Christ and a part of His mystic Self. The military fare He gives His army for the battle of life is His own Flesh and Blood. With this food and drink His members advance in holiness and courage and strength, and His Body grows in likeness to and union with its Head. Imagine an army of soldiers exactly like their Leader and compactly united with Him—such is Our Lord's army in the Mystical Body! His members are not merely under His command, not merely the King's own regiment. They always know the battle plans in His mind and the wishes of His Sacred Heart. They have not been drafted into His Company; like Peter and John they were called by His grace and they choose in love and joy to walk with Him. In His service thereafter they never work alone but as a unit, a sacred unit with our Savior helping His comrades and them helping Him. Thus in the Head and in the Body of Christ's army there reigns only the single mind of Christ, the single heart of Christ and the single spirit of Christ. We have indeed a worthy Leader who has fought in the thick of war against God's enemies and who bears His now glorious wounds as the trophy of victory. He will be with the members of His Mystical Body "all days, even to the consummation of the world"; [304] then His loyal followers will hear from their Leader's lips the well earned "At rest" with Him forever.

IV

God wishes His grace of holiness to enter each soul through Baptism, to abide there during our years on earth and to remain with us forever in Heaven. God intends the baptismal grace of divine life to be ours eternally. Even when the sinner through the priest's forgiveness recovers this grace, God still expects him to preserve it unto life everlasting.

[304] Matt. 28:20.

The Mystical Body, however, will not last forever; only on this earth does it house God's children who cling in faith and charity to their Savior. Hence a person can belong to it only from his Baptism till the moment of death; and the whole Body, as the true Church, will cease with the end of time. Yet if the Mystical Body will not endure forever, the sanctifying grace which enlivens it will live eternally in its Head, Christ, and in its members who die a holy death. Through that grace we who live and die in Christ will join our Father's family in Heaven and will possess God in everlasting love.

The sacraments give, preserve and increase the divine life for each Catholic and they do the very same for the Catholic Church, the mystic Christ. Baptism makes the newly baptized holy and entitles them to receive the other sacraments. It inserts new members into the Mystical Body as Holy Mother the Church gathers the new children of God unto herself and her Spouse, Jesus. Confirmation is the sacrament of youthful vitality. It grants Catholics a richer grace-life and through it the Mystical Body remains ever new, ever alive with divine vitality and ever powerful in defending and spreading its Catholic faith.

The Holy Eucharist is the daily Bread for God's family on earth, the one food for the whole Church. This Sacrament offers us perfect food. As the Holy Eucharist, it nourishes our souls in holiness; as food truly divine, it fosters our divine life; as the living Christ Himself, it makes each of us as well as the entire Mystical Body more Christlike. Holy Communion, the sacramental Body of Christ, remains always the perfect food for enlivening and strengthening the Mystical Body of Christ with divine life and virtue. The Eucharist, moreover, builds up charity in the Church's members so that the mutual bond of life and love between Christ and His Body becomes ever firmer while that Body, through the holiness which the Blessed Sacrament gives it, grows ever more divinely beautiful as the Bride prepared for her Spouse, Christ. The Holy Eucharist, finally, is Jesus sacramentally living on the altars of His Church at the same time that He mystically lives in His Church through grace.

In Penance our Savior offers those members of His who have sinned mortally the saving medicine which restores them to divine health of soul. This sacrament returns sinners to a firm and intimate union with their Head, Christ, and removes from other members all danger of sinful contagion. The sinner in the Mystical Body is like a branch clinging to a tree only by a thin shred of bark. These weak branches Penance regrafts onto the Vine so that the full stream of divine life again courses through them and the healthy tone of the whole Vine is increased. The branches, which sought to sever themselves from the Vine, once again clasp the living Vine which is Christ, so that the Vine is now graced with a more luxuriant growth of branches.

But the Mystical Christ has yet another medicine for His members. Through His priests He anoints those who are gravely sick in body and so saves them from the unprovided death which means eternal Hell. Holy Communion, Penance and Extreme Unction are the last sacraments we of the Mystical Body receive here; together, they speed God's children safely to their Father's home.

In Holy Orders the living Christ equips His Body with priestly leaders. The sacrament consecrates them entirely to God as holy ministers of the Mystical Body. Through the priest at Baptism, Mother Church begets new members to her Spouse, Christ. The priest guards the health of the Mystical Body. He forgives and guides his fellow members in Confession; he strengthens the brethren with priestly words; at the Lord's table he feeds God's family with the Bread of Heaven. In the Holy Sacrifice he offers Jesus, the Victim, to His heavenly Father and through that offering he, as the official minister of the Mystical Body, pays God the public worship of all Christ's members. Daily the priest leads the Good Shepherd's sheep along the paths of virtue and eternal life. Thus the priest with his sacred power is most fully another Christ; moreover, those called to the priesthood are the chief members of the Mystical Body. For they have been ordained by Jesus the official leaders of His Church. Though priests are not bound to be the holiest members of Christ, it is altogether fitting that they make their grace-life match their high rank in the Church. So will they give their brethren the tonic of good example and render themselves more fruitful in their service of the Mystical Christ.

Lastly, Matrimony takes its place among the sacraments of the Church. By making marriage between man and woman a sacrament, Jesus gave it a supernatural value and purpose. Marriage always supplied members for the human race; now, as a sacrament, it is also God's instrument for filling His Church with Catholics, the Mystical Body with other Christs, and Heaven with blessed souls. In Matrimony God's sons and daughters take up a sacred vocation to strive for holiness in the married life. Helped by the graces of their state, the wedded members of Christ rise above the standards of pagan men, do their Christian duty as parents, make the needed sacrifices gladly and let their faith settle every issue of family life. By offering their newly born to God in Baptism, Catholic parents add new members to the mystic Christ; by training their children to holiness through their counsel and example, these parents increase the depth of virtue in the Mystical Body. How vital is this religious training of the young by Christian parents, Pope Pius XII proves to us when he writes that, without it, the "Mystical Body would be in grave danger." [305] Thus, while they themselves live a life of union in Christ, Catholic fathers and mothers fulfill their vocation to the married state; at the same time they show their little ones how to take their own place as members of the mystic Jesus, so that the Mystical Body can continue through the ages. In the Church husbands and wives are not mere men and women but other Christs; they are the married members of Christ; they adorn His Mystical Body with the virtues of family life; they foster the Christ-life in their children. "Indeed, let this be clearly understood, especially in these our days: the fathers and mothers of families . . . occupy an honorable . . . place in the

[305] Encyclical *Mystici Corporis Christi.*

Christian community." [306] That community is Christ's Mystical Body.

In the living Body of Christ, which is His Church, the sacraments are life-giving. Their work keeps that Body supernaturally vigorous and healthy. Through the years Matrimony and Baptism combine to give it fresh members, alive both with human life and with the divine life of grace. Confirmation groups these members as today's apostles under their Master. In Holy Communion Jesus nourishes our grace-life with His own divine Flesh and Blood; thus His Mystical Body grows in Eucharistic love and devotion. Any weakness in the soul-life of Christ's members Penance and Extreme Unction repair, so that the divine life will course more strongly through every part of the Mystical Body. Holy Orders, finally, gives the Mystical Body its anointed leaders who, with Christ, will teach, rule and sanctify their fellow members.

Truly, everything the sacraments do for the Mystical Body is life-giving. In the new members of that Body, Baptism causes the Holy Ghost to dwell—the Spirit of Jesus who acts as the vital link uniting members and Head to each other in one Christhood. The sacramental graces, when used, adorn the Mystical Body with the beauty and power of virtue at work—the apostle's courage; the penitent's sorrow for and hatred of sin; the family virtues—self-sacrifice, love and Eucharistic devotion; priestly zeal and recollection; the virtues of perseverance in holiness—humility, faith, prayerfulness, charity and obedience. "The Savior of mankind out of His infinite goodness has provided in a marvelous way

[306] *Ibid.*

for His Mystical Body, endowing it with sacraments; so that by so many consecutive graduated graces, as it were, its members should be supported from the cradle to life's last breath." [307] In regard to the Christ-life of the Mystical Body, the sacraments are, under our Head, life-givers, life-repairers, life-strengtheners and life-builders.

V

In the Mystical Body the glorified Christ, now in Heaven, is our Head. We of His Church unite with Him to form His mystical Self. Each of us is an extension and continuation of Christ in the flesh; together with Him we make up the mystical Christ. Under Him each of us is another Christ; united, we form the new and complete Christ of the New Testament.

Jesus, our Head, is the Son of man and the Son of God; we too are children of men by birth from our human parents, and children of God through Baptism. In this twofold sonship we resemble Our Lord, but here we shall note especially our divine childhood. Christ is the first-born Son of God; we are God's younger children. Christ enjoys in the fullest the life of divine sonship; by God's grace we also live the life of divine sonship. We and Christ, then, form the family of God's children on earth. We, the offspring of God, are linked by the common bond of divine childhood. Each of us— Christ and ourselves—bears the image of our heavenly Father, as true sons should. Each of us reflects the holi-

[307] *Ibid.*

ness of our divine Father. Indeed, because Jesus perfectly mirrors God the Father, each of us bears the likeness also of Christ, our Head. Behold, then, a group living as sons of God—the group as a unit mirroring the divine life of Christ, its Head, and vitally united with Him through the grace of holiness! That group, which we call the mystical Christ, is the new Christ, the new Son of God on earth. Jesus, the Son of God, is completed by Catholics as other children of God to form the mystical Son of God.

Thus, as in each member of the Mystical Body the Father sees His child and another Christ, so in the living group He beholds His mystical Son, Jesus. This new Son shares in the likeness of God's first-born, for it is enlivened by the Spirit of Christ and mirrors our Savior's holiness and virtues. By constantly bearing and portraying that likeness to Christ before men, the new Son of God challenges and inspires others to receive the divine life of grace, to take up the divine sonship and to join the divine family. So is the mystical Son ever about His Father's business. Hence the Father is well pleased with this, His Son of the New Testament, as He was with Jesus in the flesh. Within the Blessed Trinity the Holy Spirit links the Father and the Son in one Godhead; within the Mystical Body the Holy Spirit vitally binds all the members into one divine sonship. Through the Holy Spirit the Father and the Son love each other in infinite affection; through the same Spirit God the Father and His mystical Son love each other in boundless charity. The divine family on earth, the mystical

Son of God, does indeed bear a likeness to, and entertain a familiar intimacy with, the Blessed Trinity.

While Catholics are God's children, they are also sons of our Blessed Mother, Mary. In this they again resemble Our Lord. Moreover, as the group of Catholics on earth unites with the Savior to form the mystical Son of God, that same group unites with Jesus to become the mystical Son of Mary. The Mystical Body of Christ is Mary's Child; she is the Mother of that Body.

Mary was a member of the Mystical Body from its very beginning on Calvary until she became a citizen of Heaven through her Assumption. Now, while she belongs to the Communion of Saints, she is not, strictly speaking, a member of the Mystical Body, for she no longer lives on earth. Yet because Our Lady plays a part in the Mystical Body not unlike a member's (because she is its Mother), we may in a unique and less technical sense consider her as a member of the Mystical Body. It would be unfitting to exclude a Mother from membership in her family.

Mary exercised her motherly office toward the Mystical Body even before that actually started. By freely consenting to be the Mother of God in the flesh she gave us Christ, who would thenceforth be linked to us in the Mystical Body by the bond of a common human nature, who would be our Head and who would be with us all days unto the consummation of the world. Then for thirty years Mary watched over her Son with a mother's care. On Calvary, when the Mystical Body was born, Mary was present like a true mother. She would be an honored member in it during her remaining years and she would be its Mother for all time. Under the Cross she stood, enduring her Passion with the Redeemer. In turn He willed to accept her sufferings, to join them with His own, to let her share under Himself in the work of redemption so that she became the Co-redemptrix of all mankind. Such motherly sacrifices did Mary make in behalf of her other children, her mystical Son! She suffers as a mother united in pain with her First-born—their Sacred Hearts at one in the holy purpose of bringing the divine grace-life to the Mystical Body. Mary gave us Jesus as the Savior who earned all grace for men; hence God allows all these graces to come from Christ to us through our Blessed Mother. "Therefore truly and properly may we assert that by God's wish nothing at all of that enormous treasure of grace won by Our Lord is distributed to us except through Mary." [308]

From its start Our Lord, even in death on Calvary, was the Head of the newborn Mystical Body and Mary was its Mother. Thenceforth her motherly influence was felt daily. After our Savior's Ascension she was a tower of strength and a bulwark of confidence to her new family. Moreover, by her prayers to Our Lord she won for the infant Church the descent of the Holy Ghost. On Pentecost she was present as the Mystical Body came to full life under the Holy Spirit's tongues of fire. While the Spirit of Jesus illumined and strengthened the Mystical Body, enriched it with His gifts, made it known before man and readied it for immediate action on its divine mission, Mary rejoiced in all this as the fruit of a mother's prayers for her mystical Son.

[308] Leo XIII, Encyclical *Octobri mense adventante.*

Today Mary still remains the Mother of the Mystical Body. Over the years she cherishes and fosters her mystical Son as she did her Son in the flesh. She helped prepare Jesus for His mission as the Savior of mankind; she helps the Mystical Body to carry on Christ's mission of saving the souls He redeemed. At Cana she inspired Our Lord to work His first miracle; by her holy life she inspires the mystic Christ to ever richer holiness. While she lived on earth, her virtuous deeds added to the growth and beauty of the Mystical Body; she still aids her mystical Son to grow in holiness and virtues and numbers. Just as Mary's prayers merited the descent of the Holy Ghost at Pentecost, so down the centuries has she always won the graces that mean life and increase for the Mystical Body.

Of Mary as our true Mother we can well use the prayerful words: "Never was it known that anyone who fled to thy protection, implored thy help or sought thy intercession, was left unaided." Her appearances and messages to men show her motherly desire to save her mystical Child. At Lourdes she told Bernadette: "I am the Immaculate Conception" and thereby confirmed that doctrine for the Church. Mary still crushes the serpent's head. "Thou alone hast vanquished all heresies in the whole world." [309] Thus has our Mother saved the faith of the Church in Our Lord's teachings. Mary's scapulars clothe the Mystical Body with her protecting mantle. In 1830 she revealed to St. Catherine Labouré, a Daughter of Charity, the medal which her children call "the Miraculous Medal" and promised great graces to those

[309] Office, Common of B.V.M., 7th Antiphon, Matins.

who would wear it. Through this practice the Mystical Body has advanced in devotion to its Immaculate Mother and enjoys the rich graces she promised. At Lourdes Mary has for a century honored her mystical Son with miracles of grace, courage, patience under pain and fidelity to God's will. Through the children of Fatima Mary with a mother's heart urges men to prayer and penance so that she may be able to avert war from mankind, convert Russia and save her Son's Church. A true mother gives life and fosters its growth; Mary, Mother of the Mystical Body, labors without ceasing to build the Christ-life of the mystical Jesus, her Son in His members.

Once a parent, always a parent! The Mystical Body is ever the child both of God and of Mary. It is God's family on earth and also Mary's. What a glory that the mystical Christ has God as Father and Mary as Mother! Wise is that Body when it thinks, loves, obeys, acts and lives as a child of the Father and a child of our Blessed Mother!

VI

We have learned that the divine life of grace in a person is a Christ-life. Now we would say the same about the Catholic Church, the Mystical Body of Christ. The grace-life in each member of that body is a Christ-life; the group life of the Mystical Body is also a true Christ-life.

Within the Mystical Body, Catholics who have been baptized, who profess the Catholic faith and who give obedience to the Catholic Church, are joined to Jesus in a living sacred union. Such Catholics form a Body of which Jesus is the Head. Baptism makes men Christians, that is, followers of Christ; vitally united with their Head, these Christians make up the full mystical Christ.

The divine life of the Mystical Body is a Christ-life, first, because it draws that life from Christ alone. The grace-life, vivifying the entire Mystical Body, comes, under God, only from Jesus. That is why we call Him our Head. When a man is baptized, we say he has been christened. For he has received the Christ-life, become another Christ, put on Christ; he is joined to the Mystical Body of Christ and therein starts to live his Christ-life with the entire group of Christians. So does the Christ-life constantly thrive in the Mystical Body.

With that Body, moreover, Our Lord ever remains, as He promised,[310] till the end of time. In Holy Communion He gives Himself as living food and drink to the Mystical Body the world over. Daily His Eucharistic Body nourishes and enlarges the Christ-life in His Mystical Body. Through each hour of the day His priestly members offer and receive His Flesh and Blood at the altar of sacrifice. Year in and year out the sacramental Jesus abides in our tabernacles to strengthen the Catholic life of His Church.

Yes, Jesus is the centre of life for His Mystical Body. He remains with us not only sacramentally in the Eucharist but also mystically in His Church. St. Paul prays "that Christ may dwell by faith in your hearts." [311] The Apostle prays that the faithful in Ephesus may be

310 Matt. 28:20.
311 Eph. 3:17.

vitally united with Jesus in the living oneness of the Catholic Church. St. Paul wishes the new Christians of Ephesus to be members of the Mystical Body. For there alone does Christ so dwell in men as to give them the grace-life, as to vitalize His whole mystical Self with the Christ-life. Indeed, not only does the God-man abide in His Body but His Body also abides in Him; the Vine and its branches must live in each other.[312]

And how fruitful is this mutual indwelling of Christ and Holy Mother Church! With right do they abide in each other, for Jesus is the Bridegroom who has chosen the Church as His Spouse. In His love for His Bride our Savior has crowned her with divine gifts that enable her to carry on His work of sanctifying and saving men. He has left her the fountains whence she can draw for herself the Christ-life—fountains such as the receiving of the sacraments, the offering of the Holy Sacrifice and the power to do virtuous deeds, to pray, to give alms, to practice penance and to obey the Commandments. Furthermore, Jesus protects His Spouse through all time. "Christ also loved the Church and delivered himself up for it: that he might sanctify it, cleansing it by the laver of water in the word of life: that he might present it to himself a glorious church, not having spot or wrinkle or any such thing: but that it should be holy and without blemish." [313]

In a return of love, the Church cherishes Christ as hers alone. She trusts herself to Him, she depends on Him for her Christ-life. Out of love she seeks to do the will of

[312] John 15:4–6.
[313] Eph. 5:25–27.

Christ; she bends all her strength to His service; she works to portray and to honor her Bridegroom before mankind. In their mutual espousal Jesus and His Church labor so that other Christs may be born, so that the mystical family may grow in numbers and in holiness.

We have observed the mutual indwelling of Jesus and His Church. But the Church is the Mystical Body, whose Head is Christ. So in noting the mutual bond between our Savior and the Church, we are really speaking of the mutual bond joining Christ and His Mystical Body. Between Christ, the Head, and His Body there is an intimate living union, as between the head and the other parts of a man's body; there is an abiding union as Christ dwells in His Body through all time; there is a union that bears fruit in holiness, as between a vine and its branches; there is a mutual bond of love, as of one betrothed to another—a love guiding all the actions of Christ and His Body and uniting them ever more closely; there is a life-giving union, as from our Head the Christ-life continually flows to vitalize the entire Mystical Body. "Christ . . . is your life" [314] is true also of the Mystical Body. Only Christ, our Head, instills the Christ-life into the Mystical Body. That is why we call it the Body of Christ—and no one else's!

The divine life of the Mystical Body is a Christ-life, secondly, because the Mystical Body models itself on Christ. The individual Catholic imitates our Savior; the Mystical Body too, as a group, unites in modelling itself on Jesus. Quite properly the human body conforms itself to the head; otherwise civil war would arise in man.

[314] Col. 3:4.

So likewise should the Mystical Body conform itself to its Head. On His Body, the Church, Jesus has bestowed and still bestows gifts such as He Himself had in His Christ-life: sanctifying grace, virtues, actual grace and His own Holy Spirit. With these gifts He has thus built in His Mystical Body a Christ-life like His own, and He wishes His Body, by using these gifts, to put on Christ ever more faithfully, to grow in the Christ-life steadily and to portray Christ clearly before men.

In carrying out this vocation, the Mystical Body constantly turns the eyes of faith on its Head and Model. With love it follows Christ from the manger at Bethlehem to the mount of the Ascension; it studies Jesus as He reveals Himself in each word and work; under the light of grace it ponders how it may model itself yet more on the virtuous Jesus, how it may further fill out its Christ-life; in prayer it begs the graces of courage and strength with which it will conform its deeds to its Head and thus be the living Jesus before mankind.

This enlarging of its Christ-life is the Mystical Body's vocation for all time. Through Catholic parents the Mystical Body trains its infant members to speak the Holy Name sacredly, to love Jesus, to pray to Him and to make Him their model always. Through its teachers— sisters, brothers, priests and laity—the Mystical Body educates its youthful members to take Christ for their ideal, to value His teachings, to frequent His sacraments, to do virtuous deeds in imitation of Him and so to live their Christ-life faithfully. Through its priestly members —who administer the sacraments, offer the Holy Sacrifice, preach to their flocks, instruct new converts to embrace the true faith and advise penitents in the confessional—the Mystical Body ever labors to enlarge the Christ-life of the faithful. Through its appointed leaders, the Holy Father and his bishops, the Mystical Body is guided in the footsteps of Jesus so that it will mirror its life on Him.

Hence we shall find a Christlike holiness in the Mystical Body. It gleams with the virtues of its model, Christ. Obedience marks the Mystical Body as, like Jesus, it continues to do the will of our heavenly Father. The Catholic Church is an army of worshipers, it is the mystic Christ ever adoring God three in one. It is a Body praying with and through Christ, who even in Heaven is "always living to make intercession for us." [315] The Mystical Body, suffering and persecuted, walks its constant Way of the Cross after its thorn-crowned Head. In meekness and humility it imitates the Sacred Heart of Our Lord, who told us to "learn of me because I am meek and humble of heart." [316] The charity of Christ for His brethren still drives [317] His Body on to toil unsparingly for souls. The Church accepts the truth Christ preached; bravely it speaks that truth to all men, strong and weak; boldly it spreads that truth everywhere; in defense of that truth it suffers with the courageous Christ of Calvary, condemned to die for the truth "because he made himself the Son of God." [318] To our Blessed Mother the Mystical Body, as her child, still offers the tender devotion she received from her First-

[315] Heb. 7:25.
[316] Matt. 11:29.
[317] II Cor. 5:14.
[318] John 19:7.

born. Lastly, the mystic Christ loves the triune God with a love consecrated to His service, even as on earth our Savior loved His divine Father.

Yes, the holiness of Christ ever shines forth in His Mystical Body; it must be so, since we form the Body of Christ. Behold, then, the new Christ in His Church, the one Christ still marked by a diversity of virtues. The Mystical Body unites in imitating the perfection and beauty of the virtues which Jesus practiced while on earth. Thus does the Mystical Body live and enlarge its Christ-life as through the years it follows its divine Model. Indeed, the Mystical Body considers itself blessed in being able to enjoy the Christ-life and to advance that life by imitating Jesus.

The Mystical Body lives a Christ-life, thirdly, because it carries on Christ's work among men. The characters with which the sacraments of Baptism, Confirmation and Orders seal our souls dedicate us to the service of the Savior. The Mystical Body as a group is likewise consecrated to continuing the work of the Savior throughout time.

Our Lord called Himself "the way and the truth." [319] We say the Mystical Body also is the way and the truth because it is Christ Himself. Thus by being for men what Jesus was, the Mystical Body extends His redeeming work down the centuries.

The Mystical Body is the way. The Catholic Church is the way appointed by Christ for those who would follow Him into life eternal. The true Church is the path men must walk who seek faith, holiness and salva-

[319] John 14:6.

tion in Christ. "No man cometh to the Father but by me," [320] said Jesus; so too is the Mystical Body the road from earth to Heaven.

The Mystical Body is the living truth Our Lord left to men. Jesus revealed many sublime doctrines; from its Head the Church receives them as hers alone by divine right, and through the ages she preserves them unsullied. She embodies Our Lord's teachings in her words, in her labor for souls, in her sacred rites and in her life as the Mystical Body of Christ; and she guards them so faithfully that she always possesses them as a precious treasure whence all mankind may draw. These doctrines are the saving words of Christ which men must believe, and they form the true faith which the Mystical Body ever professes before the world. Jesus called Himself "the truth"; the mystical Christ is still the truth to be embraced by all men.

While the Mystical Body remains the one answer to men's search for the true religion, it is also the teacher of religious truth. Indeed, it is man's rightful instructor, commissioned by Our Lord Himself: "Going, therefore, teach all nations." [321] For classroom the Mystical Body has the whole earth, for pupils all races of all times. The Catholic Church is the only body divinely fitted to understand, study, explain and accurately assert the sacred doctrines of her Founder. Spreading divine truth everywhere, she is the world's greatest teacher. In homes, schools, seminaries and pulpits, in books and in the writings of bishops and popes the Mystical Body teaches

[320] John 14:6.
[321] Matt. 28:19.

191

the Christian religion in order to convince men of God and of Christ, "that they may know thee, the only true God, and Jesus Christ whom thou hast sent." [322] The Mystical Body always speaks with the voice of Christ, the Teacher of men.

The Mystical Body is the light of the world. In this Body live Christ, "the light," [323] and His members, who "are the light of the world." [324] Justly then do we call the Mystical Christ the light of mankind. Because the Mystical Body teaches every doctrine Christ taught, it glows with the light of truth, which illumines for men the way to Heaven; because it does Christlike deeds, it glows with the light of holiness, which will draw souls to it and to God. For all time the Mystical Body stands like a lighthouse, beaming a shaft of light to all men around the circle of the earth. It shines forth to draw men from the darkness of ignorance and hate and unbelief and sin. With its divine light the Mystical Body illuminates its own outward features so that they can be seen by men and can attract men to Our Lord's Church. The Catholic Church will even suffer to prevent men from dimming its light; it will work all days to make its light shine for men ever more clearly, ever more brilliantly. For, like Christ Himself, the Mystical Body is "the true light which enlighteneth every man that cometh into this world." [325] It is the one light divinely fitted and commissioned to guide men to God, the living flame of

[322] John 17:3.
[323] John 8:12.
[324] Matt. 5:14.
[325] John 1:9.

divine truth and holiness ever highlighting for mankind the way to the Father.

Again like our Savior, the Mystical Body is the mediator between man and God. A mediator reconciles enemies and unites them as friends. Sin had insulted God and made men His enemies; by His Passion Jesus appeased God, won forgiveness of our sins and returned men to the divine friendship. "And therefore he is the mediator of the New Testament." [326] Today the Mystical Body, continuing Our Lord's labors, is our mediator with God. For is it not our sacred union with Christ and, through Christ, with God? Furthermore, by the prayers of its members the Mystical Body begs for men graces of forgiveness and divine intimacy. The works we do in Christ the Mystical Body offers to the Father, so that by their heavenly value they may help men live unendingly in God's friendship. Through Baptism and Penance the mystical Christ reconciles enemies of God with their Creator and returns them to the Father as His friends and children; the other sacraments foster and maintain man's loving union with God. Only one Catholic Church exists, only one Mystical Body of Christ. Yet that Body, because it is *catholic*, opens its arms to all men of all centuries. There—and there alone—can men who were enemies of each other and of God, live in union and peace within the family of God's children. Thus extending the Savior's work, the Mystical Body is our peace, our bond of union with God. In this world it is the one Mediator between man and God, the one group where men of all nations and tongues can be at

[326] Heb. 9:15.

home with each other and with the Blessed Trinity.

Lastly, the Mystical Body is Christ the Priest among men today. Indeed, it will remain throughout time the one priestly body in the world, for it, and it alone, is commissioned to continue the priestly work of Christ, its Head. However, not all the members of the Mystical Body are empowered to do that priestly work. In the human body each part performs a task which other parts cannot do; the foot cannot replace the eye. So in the Mystical Body different members perform the diverse tasks Our Lord did.[327] Only those chosen by the Church for Holy Orders are priests of God. Yet, because these ordained members truly share the priestly power of Jesus, we say that the Mystical Body itself is a priestly body. So over the years does the Catholic Church keep alive the priesthood of Jesus among His fellow men.

According to St. Paul,[328] the priest is a man divinely chosen to offer sacrifice. The Church, as the priestly Mystical Body of Christ, offers the one sacrifice pleasing to God—the Sacrifice of the Mass. In this holy rite the Mystical Body through its ordained members offers Jesus as a Victim to our heavenly Father. For the priest is the public representative of the Mystical Body. He, and he only, has been ordained to exercise the Church's power of priesthood. He, and he only, has been especially consecrated by the Church to serve as her official minister at the altar of our Eucharistic Lord. Hence, whenever the priest celebrates Mass, the Holy Sacrifice is the collective sacrifice of the entire Mystical

[327] Rom. 12:4-8.
[328] Heb. 5:1.

Body; and Jesus, the Victim most acceptable to God, is the Church's official gift to the Father. At each Mass all the other members of the Mystical Body, with minds and hearts united in common desire and prayer, join in their priest's sacrificial oblation of Christ to God. Thus through His priests, spread over the whole earth, the mystical Christ offers the one true sacrifice every moment of every day till the end of time—a perpetual sacrifice of praise and petition and thanks and reparation. The one priesthood in the world today is the priesthood of Christ; and the one group which preserves and exercises that priesthood is the Mystical Body of Christ.

We have now seen why the life of the Mystical Body is a Christ-life. The Mystical Body draws its life only from Christ, the Fountainhead of man's divine life. In duty, then, the Mystical Body models itself on Christ in order to enlarge its Christ-life. Lastly, the Body of Christ fittingly continues through time the Savior's work for souls. Since that Body is the mystical Christ, its divine life is, properly, a Christ-life.

Concerning himself the Apostle of the Gentiles wrote: "For me to live is Christ." [329] People say "My life is nursing," "My family is my life." They call that object their "life" which holds first place in their hearts. As for St. Paul, so for the Mystical Body "to live is Christ." Jesus so captivates the Mystical Body that all its energy is centered on His cause and all its toil is wrapped up in His holy purposes. The Mystical Body lives for Christ alone; and if it works for men, it thereby honors our Savior. Through the centuries the Mystical Body

[329] Phil. 1:21.

labors and suffers for one end—that mankind may know Christ, love Christ and live in Christ. For the Mystical Body cherishes Christ; it is wrapped up in Him; He holds its attention every moment; for Him the Mystical Body spends every particle of its strength.

If the Mystical Body glories in saying "for me to live is Christ," it can just as truly say "Christ liveth in me." [330] It has Jesus Christ for its Head; indeed, He is its whole life. It is the mystical Christ Himself. It is the living Christ of the New Testament, Christ mystically living in the world today. The Mystical Body is the earthly family of Christ's heavenly Father, the household of Christ's brothers and sisters, the home of other Christs. It is Jesus living in His brethren, the new child of Mary and the temple wherein the Spirit of Christ loves to dwell. It is the Church, carrying on through time Christ's labor for souls. It is the authoritative voice of Christ for all men, the praying Christ among His own and the living way to Christ in Heaven. The Mystical Body is the elected vessel of Christ's priesthood among men, the tabernacle of the sacramental Christ, the guardian of Christ's sacrifice, the priest who offers Jesus as a Victim for mankind. It is the mirror of Christ's holiness, the treasure-house of our Christ-life and the sanctuary of our divine life.

[330] Gal. 2:20.

A NOTE ON THE TYPE

IN WHICH THIS BOOK IS SET

This book is set in Janson, a Linotype face, created from the early punches of Anton Janson, who settled in Leipzig around 1670. This type is not an historic revival, but rather a letter of fine ancestry, remodelled and brought up to date to satisfy present day taste. It carries a feeling of being quite compact and sturdy. It has good color and displays a pleasing proportion of ascenders and descenders as compared to the height of the lower case letters. The book was composed and printed by the York Composition Company, Inc., of York, Pa., and bound by Moore and Company of Baltimore. The typography and design are by Howard N. King.